200 chicken dishes

hamlyn | all colour cookbook

200 chicken dishes

Sara Lewis

For Alice, who enthusiastically ate her way through all the recipes and who will, I hope, try cooking them too!

An Hachette UK Company
www.hachette.co.uk

First published in Great Britain in 2009 by Hamlyn,
a division of Octopus Publishing Group Ltd,
Endeavour House, 189 Shaftesbury Avenue,
London WC2H 8JY
www.octopusbooks.co.uk

ISBN: 978-0-600-61859-1

A CIP catalogue record for this book is available from the British Library

Printed and bound in China

3 4 5 6 7 8 9 10

Both metric and imperial measurements are given for the recipes. Use one set of measures only, not a mixture of both.

Standard level spoon measures are used in all recipes:
1 tablespoon = one 15 ml spoon
1 teaspoon = one 5 ml spoon

Ovens should be preheated to the specified temperature. If using a fan-assisted oven, follow the manufacturer's instructions for adjusting the time and temperature.

Poultry should be cooked thoroughly. To test if poultry is cooked, pierce the flesh through the thickest part with a skewer or fork – the juices should run clear, never pink or red.

Eggs should be medium unless otherwise stated; choose free-range if possible and preferably organic. The Department of Health advises that eggs should not be consumed raw. This book contains some dishes made with raw or lightly cooked eggs. It is prudent for more vulnerable people, such as pregnant and nursing mothers, invalids, the elderly, babies and young children, to avoid uncooked or lightly cooked dishes made with eggs.

This book includes dishes made with nuts and nut derivatives. It is advisable for those with known allergic reactions to nuts and nut derivatives and those who may be potentially vulnerable to these allergies, such as pregnant and nursing mothers, invalids, the elderly, babies and children, to avoid dishes made with nuts and nut oils. It is also prudent to check the labels of prepared ingredients for the possible inclusion of nut derivatives.

contents

introduction

introduction

As you push your trolley around the supermarket for your weekly food shop, you will probably add one or two packs of chicken, perhaps a pack of boneless, skinless breasts, some thighs or a whole chicken, not forgetting mini breast fillets, minced chicken, chicken livers or drumsticks. The different cuts cover a wide range of prices, so there is something for every budget. But it is all too easy to go into 'automatic pilot', as we juggle hectic workloads, family commitments and daily chores, and just cook the same old recipes. Chicken is highly versatile, and with 200 recipes to choose from in this book we hope that you will be able to add some new favourites to your family's repertoire.

Much has been made in the media about the welfare of chickens during rearing. For those on a tight budget, battery-farmed chickens may be the only option. Try to use up the leftovers the following day, or use the redundant carcass to make stock, so that a more expensive free-range chicken, even if not organic, is more cost-effective. While organic, free-range chickens may not be for everyone, try to choose whole chickens and chicken joints with labels indicating that the birds have been reared humanely (for more information, consult the RSPCA in the UK or the HSUS in the USA).

The recipes in this book have been grouped into chapters so that you can quickly find one to suit your needs, whether it be for a light snack, some party food or a full evening meal. When you are really short of time you can choose from Gingered Chicken with Soft noodles (see page 20), Seared Chicken & Vegetable Wraps (see page 56) or Peppered Chicken & Aubergines (see page 140), all ready including preparation and cooking within 30 minutes. For an easy midweek supper what about chillied Chicken Arrabiata (see page 84), Blackened Chicken & Beans (see page 116) or Thai Sesame Chicken Patties (see page 118)? For something a little more traditional there are Chicken, Bacon & Sage Meatballs (see page 130) or Chicken Thatch (see page 132), the poultry version of Shepherds Pie.

If it suits you better then opt for a supper that requires little preparation but that can then be left in the oven to cook slowly, leaving you free to get on with something else. Chicken Stew & Dumplings (see page 96), packed with root vegetables and pearl barley simmered with pale ale or Stoved Chicken with Black Pudding (see page 120), a Scottish inspired casserole topped with sliced potatoes would fit the bill perfectly.

For a meal to share with friends why not try Chicken Mole (see page 154), a Mexican dish with chocolate or Chicken & Mushroom Lasagne (see page 164). Both can be made up earlier in the day then reheated when needed. For something to impress what about Baked Chicken in a Salt Crust with red pepper ketchup (see page 172) or Italian Chicken Cushion (see page 184), a boned whole chicken stuffed with a delicious mix of basil, sundried tomatoes and olives. For a more leisurely relaxing Sunday lunch choose one of the comforting roasts with a twist, perfect for all seasons with an option for dinner for two.

There's a whole chapter on what to do with the leftovers, from Chicken & Spinach Chowder (see page 218) to Chicken & Avocado Salad (see page 228) or Cheesy Chicken & Chutney Puffs (see page 230) that make maximum use of the leftover bits from a roast along with tips on making stock so that nothing is wasted.

Influenced by a fusion of flavours from around the world, from Thailand to the Caribbean, plain chicken will be a thing of the past. So, if you are in need of inspiration to awaken those taste buds, read on.

Hygiene essentials

- Keep raw and cooked chicken separate in the refrigerator so that raw chicken juices cannot drip on to other foods.
- Cover food dishes so that chicken does not dry out.
- Use separate boards and knives for preparing raw and cooked chicken, as well as for preparing meat and vegetables.
- Defrost frozen chicken in the refrigerator, transferring to room temperature for 1–2 hours before cooking.
- Only reheat cooked food once, and make sure it is piping hot all the way through. Don't warm foods, especially if using the microwave.
- Raw chicken that has been defrosted can only be put back in the freezer if it has been cooked and cooled. If taken out of the freezer in a cooked state, it cannot be refrozen.
- Add a small frozen ice pack to lunchboxes, and use an insulated lunchbag so that any cooked chicken stays cold.

How to make chicken stock

Why bother making your own stock? In an age when we are all being advised to cut down on our salt consumption, homemade stock can be salt-free; it also fits in with our general tendency to recycle all we can. If you haven't got time to make stock now, don't throw the chicken carcass out – just pack it into a plastic bag and freeze it until you do have time. The following recipe makes 1.4 litres (2½ pints).

chicken carcass from a roast or poached whole bird
2 litres (3½ pints) **cold water**
1 large **onion**, cut into quarters but still with the inner brown layer of skin attached
2 **carrots**, thickly sliced
2 **celery sticks**, thickly sliced
small bunch of **mixed fresh herbs** or a **dried bouquet garni**
black peppercorns

Put the chicken carcass into a large saucepan with the measured water, and add the onion, carrots and celery. Flavour with the fresh herbs or bouquet garni and a few black peppercorns, then bring to the boil. Partially cover the top of the pan with a lid, then leave to simmer gently for 2 hours. Strain into a jug and leave to cool. Store in the refrigerator for 2–3 days or freeze in handy-sized plastic containers or well-sealed plastic bags if the carcass had not already been frozen.

Preparation

Before use, always rinse chicken well in cold water, drain well and pat dry with kitchen paper; this is especially important if you are using prepacked raw chicken. When rinsing a whole chicken, take extra care to rinse inside the bird, and remove giblets if included.

If using frozen chicken, make sure it is completely defrosted before use. Don't try to speed up defrosting by plunging it into warm water. Immerse in cold water and change the water frequently, or defrost in the microwave, following the manufacturer's guidelines.

Is the chicken cooked?

Chicken must never be served rare or medium, but always well done. Insert a skewer or small knife into the thickest part of a joint, or through a thigh to the breast if cooking a whole chicken. The juices will run clear when the chicken is ready – if you see any traces of pink in the juices, continue cooking. If pan-frying or grilling, check at 5-minute intervals. For a whole chicken, re-test after 15 minutes more in the oven.

How to joint a whole chicken

This is not as tricky as it may first seem; the secret is to have a good sharp knife and locate the joints by feel before cutting through them to separate. This technique can be adapted to cut up guineafowl, turkey, duck or other poultry.

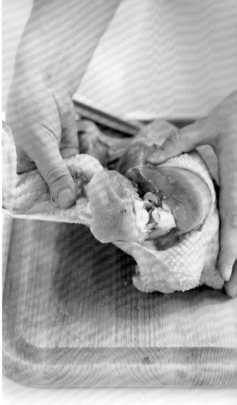

1 First remove the trussing strings and put the chicken breast side uppermost on a chopping board. Pull one leg gently away from the body. Cut through the skin between the body and leg, cut down through the meat, and then work down to the thigh joint. Bend the leg so that it eases the leg bone from its socket, then cut through the ball-and-socket joint. Repeat with the other leg.

2 To remove the wings, press one wing against the body of the bird so that both parts of the shoulder are visible. Cut through the skin, then down through the joint to sever. Tuck the wingtip under the shoulder to make a triangular shape joint. Repeat with the other wing.

3 Split the carcass by cutting around and under both breasts with poultry shears or strong kitchen scissors. Cut through the rib cage, so separating the backbone from the breasts. Repeat on the other side.

4 Cut along the centre of the breast with poultry shears, strong kitchen scissors or a sharp knife, then either slide a knife under the breast meat on each side of the bone to release two boneless breast joints or cut straight down between the breast bone with a large cook's knife to give two joints on the bone. For a 'supreme' leave the wing joint attached at step 2, but sever at the first joint so separating wing tips from body.

5 Now separate the leg joint into a drumstick and thigh. Put the joint skin side uppermost, then flex the drumstick slightly so that you can see where the central joint is. Cut through the ball-and-socket joint. Repeat with the other leg.

6 You should now have 2 drumsticks, 2 thigh joints, 2 wings and 2 breast joints, plus a carcass (not pictured) to make stock with. When the bird is small, leave the drumstick and thigh joint joined together.

How to spatchcock a chicken or poussin

Here the bird is split and then flattened so that it cooks more quickly. This enables a whole bird to be barbecued, grilled or roasted traditionally in a shorter time.

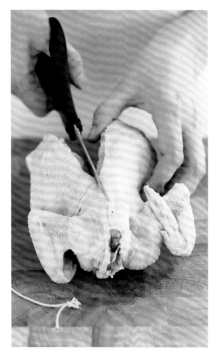

2 Turn the bird over, then using the palm of your hand press down on the breast and flatten it slightly.

3 Trim off the knuckle bones from the drumsticks and tuck the wingtips under the bird. Neaten off any untidy skin and insert two long metal or wooden skewers through each leg, breast and wing so that they cross under the bird and keep it flat during roasting or barbecuing.

1 Put the chicken or poussin breast side down on a chopping board and remove the trussing string. Cut the bird in half using poultry shears or sturdy kitchen scissors.

How to carve a roast chicken

A good carving knife and fork are essential. Choose a knife that has a long, slightly flexible blade and a fork with tines that are close together. Even more importantly, you must keep the knife sharp. If you find using a knife steel too daunting, there are many hand or electrical knife sharpeners available from good cookshops or major department stores – it really is worth investing in one. Carve off just the amounts you need at a time, working first on one side and then on the other side of the bird, as needed. If the bird is stuffed, don't forget to serve the stuffing with a spoon.

1 Put the chicken on a large chopping board or serving plate with the breast side uppermost. Steadying the joint with a carving fork, cut the skin between the breast and one thigh joint and work downwards through the meat to the joint. Bend the leg outwards to locate the thigh joint, then cut down through the joint to remove the first leg.

2 To remove the wing on the same side of the chicken, cut down through the corner of the breast to the wing joint. Flex the wing as you did for the leg to locate the joint, then cut down between the joint to remove the wing.

3 Working on the same side of the chicken, make thin diagonal cuts down the breast to slice the meat, using the fork to steady the joint and to help you to remove each slice.

4 Now that the breast has been sliced, separate the thigh and drumstick joints, then cut thin slices of meat off both joints that follow the direction of the bone.

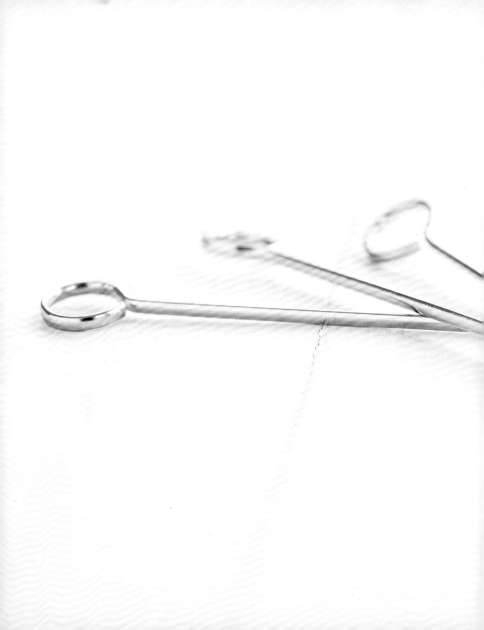

light
lunches

gingered chicken with soft noodles

Serves **4**

Preparation time **10 minutes**

Cooking time **12–13 minutes**

2 teaspoons **sesame oil**

2 teaspoons **sunflower oil**

2 boneless, skinless **chicken breasts**, diced

2 **garlic cloves**, finely chopped

2.5 cm (1 inch) piece **root ginger**, peeled, finely grated

300 g (10 oz) pack **ready-prepared stir-fry crunchy vegetables**

50 g (2 oz) **ready-salted peanuts**, roughly chopped

400 g (13 oz) pack **chilled fresh egg noodles**

2 tablespoons **sweet chilli dipping sauce**

3 tablespoons **soy sauce**

2 teaspoons **fish sauce** (optional)

small bunch **fresh coriander**, to garnish (optional)

Pour the oils into a wok or large frying pan. When hot, add the chicken and stir-fry for 5 minutes, until lightly browned. Add the garlic and ginger and cook for 1 minute.

Add the mixed vegetables and stir-fry for 3 minutes. Mix in the peanuts and the noodles and stir-fry for 2–3 minutes until hot. Add the chilli sauce, soy sauce and fish sauce, if using, and cook for 1 minute. Spoon into small bowls, and garnish with torn coriander leaves, if liked.

For gingered chicken with beansprout salad, fry the chicken as above, omitting the stir-fried vegetables and noodles, then leave to cool. Mix 125 g (4 oz) rinsed beansprouts with 1 finely shredded Cos lettuce, 1 carrot and 1 courgette, both coarsely grated. Add the chicken, peanuts and sauces and toss together. Garnish with torn coriander.

seared chicken sandwich

Serves **4**
Preparation time **15 minutes**
Cooking time **5–6 minutes**

250 g (8 oz) **mini chicken breast fillets**
8 teaspoons **balsamic vinegar**
8 slices **granary bread**
6 tablespoons **low-fat natural yogurt**
½–1 teaspoon **freshly grated hot horseradish** or **horseradish sauce**, to taste
100 g (3½ oz) **mixed salad leaves with beetroot strips**
pepper

Put the mini chicken breast fillets into a plastic bag with half the vinegar and toss together until evenly coated.

Heat a nonstick frying pan, lift the chicken out of the plastic bag with a fork and add the pieces to the pan. Fry for 3 minutes, turn and drizzle with the vinegar from the bag and cook for 2–3 more minutes or until browned and cooked through.

Toast the bread lightly on both sides. Slice the chicken into long, thin strips and arrange them on 4 slices of toast. Mix together the yogurt and horseradish and a little pepper to taste. Add the salad leaves and toss together.

Spoon the yogurt and salad leaves over the chicken, drizzle over the remaining vinegar, if liked, and top with the remaining slices of toast. Cut each sandwich in half and serve immediately.

For tangy chicken, lemon and garlic toasties,
toss the chicken fillets with the juice of ½ lemon and 1 tablespoon olive oil then fry as above but without the vinegar. Toast 8 slices wholemeal bread then spread with 4 tablespoons garlic mayonnaise. Divide the chicken between 4 slices of toast then top with the shredded leaves of 2 Little Gem lettuces and a 5 cm (2 inch) piece cucumber, thinly sliced. Cover with the remaining slices of toast then press together and cut into triangles.

quinoa salad with seared chicken

Serves **4**
Preparation time **25 minutes**
Cooking time **22 minutes**

175 g (6 oz) **quinoa**
¼ **cucumber**, finely diced
1 small **green pepper**, cored,
  deseeded, finely diced
6 **spring onions**, trimmed,
  thinly sliced
125 g (4 oz) **frozen peas**,
  just defrosted
grated rind and juice of
  1 **lemon**
2 tablespoons **olive oil**
1 tablespoon **harissa paste**
4 boneless, skinless **chicken
  breasts**, cut into long
  thin slices
small bunch **mint**, finely
  chopped

For the dressing
3 tablespoons **olive oil**
1 tablespoon **harissa paste**
grated rind and juice of
  1 **lemon**
salt

Add the quinoa to a saucepan of boiling water and simmer for about 10 minutes or according to packet instructions until just tender, then drain in a fine sieve.

Make the dressing by mixing the olive oil, harissa, lemon rind and juice and a little salt in a salad bowl. Stir in the hot quinoa and leave to cool, then mix in the cucumber, green pepper, spring onions and frozen peas.

Mix the lemon rind and juice, oil and harissa in a shallow bowl, then add the chicken and toss well. Heat a griddle pan (or ordinary frying pan), then cook the chicken in batches for about 6 minutes, turning until browned on both sides and cooked through.

Stir the mint through the quinoa salad, then top with the warm chicken. Serve warm or cold. Any leftovers can be chilled and packed into lunchboxes the following day.

For hot feta & almond quinoa with seared chicken,
toss the just-cooked quinoa in the dressing as above. Omit the cucumber, adding 1 deseeded and chopped red pepper instead, and 50 g (2 oz) sultanas and 75 g (3 oz) diced, ready-to-eat dried apricots in place of the peas. Sprinkle with 100 g (3½ oz) drained and crumbled feta cheese and 50 g (2 oz) toasted flaked almonds. Top with the chicken and serve hot with extra spoonfuls of harissa.

asian citrus chicken skewers

Serves **4**
Preparation time **5 minutes**,
  plus marinating
Cooking time **20 minutes**

500 g (1 lb) boneless, skinless
  chicken breasts, cubed
grated rind and juice of
  1 lemon
2 teaspoons **Chinese
  5-spice powder**
1 tablespoon **dark soy sauce**
mixed vegetables (carrots,
  spring onions, radishes), cut
  into strips, to serve (optional)

Place the chicken, lemon rind and juice, 5-spice powder and soy sauce in a bowl. Stir to combine, cover, then leave to marinate in the refrigerator for at least 1 hour or overnight.

Thread the chicken pieces on to 4 presoaked wooden skewers, pushing them tightly together. Grill for 10 minutes under a preheated moderate grill. Turn the skewers, baste with any remaining marinade, and grill for a further 10 minutes. Serve on a bed of vegetables, if liked.

For piri piri chicken skewers, mix the grated lemon rind and juice with 2 tablespoons olive oil then add 2 teaspoons piri piri seasoning, 2 teaspoons tomato purée and 2 cloves of finely chopped garlic. Add the chicken, marinade then grill as above.

teriyaki chicken with three seeds

Serves **4**

Preparation time **20 minutes**,
   plus marinating

Cooking time **16–20 minutes**

4 boneless, skinless **chicken
   breasts**, about 125 g (4 oz)
   each
2 tablespoons **sunflower oil**
4 tablespoons **soy sauce**
2 **garlic cloves**, finely
   chopped
2.5 cm (1 inch) piece **root
   ginger**, finely grated
2 tablespoons **sesame seeds**
2 tablespoons **sunflower
   seeds**
2 tablespoons **pumpkin
   seeds**
juice of 2 **limes**
100 g (3½ oz) **herb salad**
½ small **iceberg lettuce**,
   torn into bite-sized pieces
50 g (2 oz) **alfalfa** or **brocco**
   sprouting seeds

Put the chicken breasts into a shallow china dish.
Spoon three-quarters of the oil over the chicken,
then add half the soy sauce, the garlic and the ginger.
Turn the chicken to coat in the mixture, then leave
to marinate for 30 minutes.

Heat a nonstick frying pan, then lift the chicken
out of the marinade and add to the pan. Fry for
8–10 minutes each side until dark brown and cooked
all the way through. Lift out and set aside.

Heat the remaining oil in the pan, add the seeds and
fry for 2–3 minutes until lightly toasted. Add the
remaining marinade and remaining soy sauce, bring
to the boil, then take off the heat and mix in the
lime juice.

Mix the herb salad, lettuce and sprouting seeds
together, then spoon over 4 serving plates. Thinly slice
the chicken and arrange on top, then spoon the seed
and lime dressing over the top. Serve at once.

For teriyaki chicken with oriental salad, marinate the
chicken as above and make a salad with 200 g (7 oz)
carrots, cut into thin strips, 4 spring onions, cut into
thin strips, 6 thinly sliced radishes and ½ small head
of Chinese leaves, thinly shredded. Fry the chicken
as above, omit the seeds and then continue with
the dressing as above. Slice the chicken, arrange
on the salad and drizzle with the warm dressing.

chicken with sweet potato wedges

Serves **4**

Preparation time **20 minutes**

Cooking time **35 minutes**

4 **sweet potatoes**, about
1.25 kg (2½ lb) in total,
scrubbed

4 **chicken thighs**, boned,
skinned, cut into chunks

1 **red onion**, cut into wedges

4 **plum tomatoes**, cut into
chunks

150 g (5 oz) **chorizo** in one
piece, skinned, sliced or
diced depending on
diameter

3 stems **rosemary**, leaves torn
from stems

4 tablespoons **olive oil**

salt and **pepper**

Cut the potatoes in half, then into thick wedges, and put them into a large roasting tin with the chicken, onion and tomatoes. Tuck the chorizo in and around the potatoes, then sprinkle with the rosemary and some salt and pepper.

Drizzle with the oil, then roast in a preheated oven, 200°C (400°F), Gas Mark 6, for about 35 minutes, turning once or twice until the chicken is golden and cooked through and the potato wedges browned and tender.

Spoon on to serving plates and serve as it is, or with a watercress salad.

For mixed roots with fennel & chicken, use
1.25 kg (2½ lb) of mixed baking potatoes, parsnips and carrots. Peel the parsnips and carrots, then cut all vegetables into wedges. Add to the roasting tin with the chicken as above. Sprinkle with 2 teaspoons fennel seeds, 1 teaspoon turmeric and 1 teaspoon paprika, then drizzle with 4 tablespoons olive oil and roast as above.

spiced chicken & mango salad

Serves **4**
Preparation time **15 minutes**
Cooking time **5–6 minutes**

4 small boneless, skinless
   chicken breasts
6 teaspoons **mild curry paste**
Juice of 1 **lemon**
150 g (5 oz) **low-fat natural**
   yogurt
1 **mango**
50 g (2 oz) **watercress**
½ **cucumber**, diced
½ **red onion**, chopped
½ **iceberg lettuce**

Cut the chicken breasts into long, thin slices. Put 4 teaspoons of the curry paste in a plastic bag with the lemon juice and mix together by squeezing the bag. Add the chicken and toss together.

Half-fill the base of a steamer with water and bring to the boil. Place the chicken in the top of the steamer in a single layer, cover and steam for 5–6 minutes until thoroughly cooked. Test the chicken (see page 11).

Meanwhile, mix the remaining curry paste in a bowl with the yogurt.

Cut a thick slice off either side of the mango to reveal the large, flat stone. Trim the flesh away from the stone, then remove the peel and cut the flesh into bite-sized chunks.

Rinse the watercress with cold water and tear it into bite-sized pieces. Add to the yogurt dressing with the cucumber, red onion and mango and toss together gently.

Tear the lettuce into pieces, divide it among 4 plates, spoon the mango mixture on top and complete with the warm chicken strips.

For coronation chicken, mix the curry paste and yogurt with 4 tablespoons mayonnaise. Stir in 500 g (1 lb) cold cooked diced chicken and 40 g (1½ oz) sultanas. Sprinkle with 25 g (1 oz) toasted flaked almonds and serve on a bed of mixed salad and herb leaves.

chicken liver pâté with mushrooms

Serves **4**
Preparation time **25 minutes**,
   plus chilling
Cooking time **20 minutes**

15 g (½ oz) **dried porcini
   mushrooms**
200 ml (7 fl oz) **boiling water**
25 g (1 oz) **butter**
1 tablespoon **olive oil**
1 **red onion**, roughly chopped
227 g (7½ oz) pack **frozen
   chicken livers**, defrosted
2 **garlic cloves**, finely
   chopped
2–3 stems **thyme**, leaves torn
   from stems
6 tablespoons **red wine**
salt and **pepper**

For the butter layer
½ **red onion**, thinly sliced
thyme leaves
75 g (3 oz) **butter**

Soak the dried mushrooms in a heatproof bowl just covered with the boiling water for 15 minutes. Meanwhile, heat the butter and oil in a frying pan, add the onion and fry gently for 10 minutes until softened and just beginning to brown.

Tip the chicken livers into a sieve, rinse with cold water, drain well, then roughly chop, discarding any white cores. Add to the onions with the garlic and fry for 4–5 minutes, stirring until browned.

Add the mushrooms and their soaking liquid, the thyme leaves, red wine and some seasoning. Cover and cook for 5 minutes, then cool slightly.

Purée the liver mixture in a food processor or liquidizer until smooth. Spoon into four small dishes and level the surface.

Sprinkle the raw onion and thyme leaves over the pâté. Melt the butter in a small saucepan, tilt the pan and scoop the clear melted butter on to the pâté, discarding the cloudy white milk solids in the bottom of the pan. Cover and chill for 3–4 hours or overnight until firm. Serve with toast and rocket leaves.

For brandied chicken liver & pistachio pâté, omit the mushrooms. Add 2 tablespoons brandy to the fried chicken livers and, when bubbling, flame with a taper. Omit the red wine and add 150 ml (¼ pint) chicken stock (see page 10) along with the thyme leaves. Purée, then mix in 50 g (2 oz) sliced pistachios, saving a few for the buttery top layer.

thai red chicken & cashew sauce

Serves **2**
Preparation time **8 minutes**
Cooking time **9–12 minutes**

300 g (10 oz) boneless
　chicken thighs, thickly
　sliced
75 ml (3 fl oz) **Thai red curry
　paste**
2 **pitta breads**, split in half
　horizontally

For the cashew sauce
150 g (5 oz) **cashew nuts**,
　lightly toasted
1 teaspoon **crushed red chilli
　flakes**
50 ml (2 fl oz) **soy sauce**
250 ml (8 fl oz) **coconut milk**
50 ml (2 fl oz) **coriander
　leaves**, plus extra to garnish
2 tablespoons **palm sugar** or
　light brown sugar
2 tablespoons **rice wine
　vinegar**
2 **kaffir lime leaves**,
　shredded

To make the cashew sauce, place the nuts in a food processor and pulse until finely chopped. Place in a small pan with the remaining sauce ingredients and heat gently for 4–5 minutes, stirring frequently to prevent sticking, until the sauce is thick and glossy.

Mix the chicken slices with the red curry paste and thread on to 4 metal skewers.

Preheat a sandwich grill and lay the skewers directly on the heat, bringing down the top plate to seal the chicken. Grill for 5–6 minutes, until the chicken is thoroughly cooked. Remove from the heat and set aside.

When the meat is cool enough to handle, push the chicken off the skewers directly into the pitta breads. Toast the breads in the cleaned sandwich grill for 1–2 minutes, or according to the manufacturer's instructions, until they are crispy and the chicken hot.

Cut each pitta in half, garnish with coriander leaves and serve immediately with a bowl of the warm cashew sauce.

For Thai red chicken with lime-dressed courgettes, cook the chicken on skewers as above. While the chicken cools slightly, mix 1 tablespoon sunflower oil with the grated rind and juice of 1 lime, 2 tablespoons roughly chopped coriander and seasoning in a plastic bag. Add 2 courgettes, cut into thin lengthwise slices and toss in the bag. Lift out with a fork and add to the sandwich grill, then cook until lightly browned. Arrange on plates, drizzle with the remaining dressing and top with the chicken. Serve with rice.

griddled chicken & fennel pockets

Serves **4**

Preparation time **15 minutes**

Cooking time **9–10 minutes**

450 g (14 oz) **mini chicken breast fillets**, thinly sliced

1 **fennel bulb**, thinly sliced

2 tablespoons **olive oil**

2 **garlic cloves**, finely chopped

4 **pitta breads**

2 **oranges**, peeled, cut into segments

40 g (1½ oz) **watercress**

salt and **pepper**

For the dressing

2 tablespoons **low-fat natural yogurt**

1 teaspoon **wholegrain mustard**

1 teaspoon **runny honey**

salt and **pepper**

Toss the chicken and fennel with the oil, garlic and a little seasoning. Preheat a griddle pan (or ordinary frying pan), then add the pitta breads and cook for 1–2 minutes, turning until hot and puffy. Remove from the pan and keep hot.

Add the chicken and fennel to the pan and fry for about 8 minutes, turning once until browned and cooked through. Meanwhile, make the dressing by mixing the yogurt with the mustard, honey and a little seasoning.

Slit the pitta breads and fill with the orange segments, watercress, chicken and fennel, then drizzle the dressing over and serve immediately.

For chicken pittas with carrot salad, fry the chicken with oil and garlic as above but omit the fennel. Mix 2 tablespoons olive oil with 2 teaspoons wholegrain mustard, the juice of ½ orange and seasoning, then stir in 2 grated carrots, 2 tablespoons sultanas and a small handful of torn coriander. Divide between warmed pittas and add the chicken.

devilled chicken

Serves **4**
Preparation time **10 minutes**
Cooking time **16–20 minutes**

8 boneless **chicken thighs**
salad leaves, to serve

For the devil sauce
2 tablespoons **Dijon mustard**
6 drops **Tabasco sauce**
2 **garlic cloves**, crushed
1 tablespoon **soy sauce**

Heat a large griddle pan (or ordinary frying pan). Remove the skin from the chicken thighs, open them out and trim away any fat.

To make the devil sauce, mix together the mustard, Tabasco, garlic and soy sauce in a shallow dish.

Dip the trimmed chicken thighs in the devil sauce and coat each piece well. Place the chicken pieces flat on the pan and cook for 8–10 minutes on each side.

Serve hot or cold with salad leaves.

For jerk chicken, mix 3 tablespoons jerk marinade (a ready-made paste) with the grated rind and juice of ½ an orange and 2 finely chopped cloves of garlic. Dip the chicken in this mixture then cook as above. Serve with a rice or a salad.

warm chicken salad with anchovies

Serves **4**
Preparation time **20 minutes**
Cooking time **11–14 minutes**

150 g (5 oz) **green beans**,
  thickly sliced
1 small **crisp lettuce**, leaves
  separated and torn into
  pieces
6 **spring onions**, thinly sliced
175 g (6 oz) **cherry
  tomatoes**, halved
275 g (9 oz) jar **mixed
  pepper antipasto in oil**
2 boneless, skinless **chicken
  breasts**, diced
50 g (2 oz) **fresh
  breadcrumbs**
4 canned **anchovy fillets**,
  drained, chopped

For the dressing
3 tablespoons **olive oil**
2 teaspoons **sun-dried
  tomato paste**
4 teaspoons **red wine vinegar**
salt and **pepper**

Blanch the green beans in a saucepan of boiling water for 3–4 minutes until just tender. Drain, rinse with cold water and drain again.

Put the beans, lettuce, onions and tomatoes into a large salad bowl. Lift the peppers out of the jar, reserving the oil, dice if needed and add to the salad.

Pour 2 tablespoons oil from the pepper jar into a frying pan, add the chicken and fry for 8–10 minutes, stirring until golden and cooked through. Spoon over the salad. Heat 1 tablespoon extra oil in the pan, add the breadcrumbs and anchovies, and stir-fry until golden.

Mix the dressing ingredients together, toss over the salad, then sprinkle with the breadcrumbs and anchovies and serve immediately.

For chicken Caesar salad, mix the green beans with the lettuce, 4 hardboiled eggs cut into wedges, spring onions and lettuce as above, plus 4 chopped anchovy fillets. Cut 75 g (3 oz) bread into cubes and fry in 2 tablespoons olive oil and 25 g (1 oz) butter. Mix 4 tablespoons mayonnaise with 1 finely chopped garlic clove and the juice of 1 lime. Toss with the salad, then sprinkle with croutons and 40 g (1½ oz) grated Parmesan cheese.

griddled summer chicken salad

Serves **4**

Preparation time **15 minutes**

Cooking time **45 minutes**

4 x 125 g (4 oz) boneless,
   skinless **chicken breasts**

2 small **red onions**

2 **red peppers**, cored,
   deseeded, cut into flat pieces

1 bunch **asparagus**, trimmed

200 g (7 oz) **new potatoes**,
   boiled, cut in half

1 bunch **basil**

5 tablespoons **olive oil**

2 tablespoons **balsamic
   vinegar**

salt and **pepper**

Heat a griddle pan (or ordinary frying pan). Place the chicken breasts in the pan and cook for 8–10 minutes on each side. When cooked, remove from the pan and cut roughly into chunks.

Cut the red onions into wedges, keeping the root ends intact to hold the wedges together. Place in the pan and cook for 5 minutes on each side. Remove from the pan and set aside.

Place the flat pieces of red pepper in the pan and cook for 8 minutes on the skin side only, so that the skins are charred and blistered. Remove and set aside, then cook the asparagus in the pan for 6 minutes, turning frequently.

Put the boiled potatoes in a large bowl. Tear the basil, reserving a few leaves intact to garnish, and add to the bowl, together with the chicken and all the vegetables. Add the olive oil, balsamic vinegar and seasoning. Toss the salad and garnish with the reserved basil leaves.

For summer chicken wraps, omit the potatoes and make the recipe up as above. Warm 4 soft tortillas as directed on the pack then spread with 200 g (7 oz) hummus. Toss the griddled chicken, cut into strips, and vegetables with 2 tablespoons olive oil, the balsamic vinegar as above and reserved basil leaves. Divide between the tortillas then roll up tightly and serve cut in half while the chicken is still warm.

barbecued chicken with apple slaw

Serves **4**
Preparation time **25 minutes**
Cooking time **15 minutes**

6 tablespoons **tomato
    ketchup**
2 tablespoons **Worcestershire
    sauce**
2 tablespoons **red wine
    vinegar**
2 tablespoons **light
    muscovado sugar**
2 teaspoons **English mustard**
12 **chicken wings**

For the apple slaw
1 **dessert apple**, cored, diced
1 tablespoon **lemon juice**
1 **carrot**, coarsely grated
3 **spring onions**, thinly sliced
200 g (7 oz) **white cabbage**,
    finely shredded, core
    discarded
6 tablespoons **light
    mayonnaise**
salt and **pepper**

Mix the ketchup, Worcestershire sauce, vinegar, sugar and mustard together. Put the chicken on a foil-lined baking sheet or grill rack, then brush with the ketchup mixture.

Cook the chicken wings under a preheated grill or on a barbecue for about 15 minutes, turning once or twice until a deep brown and the chicken is cooked through. Test the chicken (see page 11).

Meanwhile, mix all the slaw ingredients together in a bowl, then spoon into a bowl. Put the chicken wings on to a plate and serve with plenty of paper napkins for sticky fingers.

For Chinese barbecued chicken wings, mix 4 tablespoons hoisin sauce with 4 tablespoons orange juice, 2 tablespoons Chinese rice wine or dry sherry and 2 tablespoons tomato ketchup. Brush over the chicken and grill or barbecue as above.

chicken club sandwich

Serves **4**

Preparation time **15 minutes**

Cooking time **10 minutes**

4 small boneless, skinless **chicken breasts**, thinly sliced

8 rashers **smoked streaky bacon**

1 tablespoon **sunflower oil**

12 slices **bread**

4 tablespoons **light mayonnaise**

125 g (4 oz) **dolcelatte or bleu d'Auvergne cheese**, thinly sliced

4 **tomatoes**, thinly sliced

40 g (1½ oz) **watercress**

Fry the chicken and bacon in the oil for 6–8 minutes, turning once or twice until golden and the chicken is cooked through.

Toast the bread on both sides, then spread with the mayonnaise. Divide the chicken and bacon between four slices of toast, then top with the sliced cheese. Cover the cheese with 4 more slices of toast, then add the tomato slices and watercress. Complete the sandwich stacks with the final slices of toast.

Press the sandwiches together, then cut each stack into 4 small triangles. Secure with cocktail sticks, if needed, and serve immediately.

For deli deluxe chicken sandwich, fry the chicken in the oil as above, omitting the bacon. Split and toast the cut sides of a ciabatta loaf, spread the lower half with 4 teaspoons of black-olive tapenade, then top with 2 tablespoons of mayonnaise. Add the chicken to the tapenade toast, cover with 125 g (4 oz) sliced brie cheese, then 75 g (3 oz) sun-dried tomatoes and 40 g (1½ oz) rocket leaves. Top with the remaining toast, then cut into 4 thick slices. Serve warm.

chicken with peanut sauce

Serves **4**
Preparation time **5 minutes**
Cooking time **16–20 minutes**

4 x 125 g (4 oz) boneless,
  skinless **chicken breasts**
1 tablespoon **soy sauce**
2 tablespoons **crunchy or
  smooth peanut butter**
4 tablespoons **lemon juice**
4 tablespoons **water**
pepper

To garnish
coriander leaves
peanuts, fried, chopped
  (optional)

Heat a griddle pan (or ordinary frying pan). Place the chicken breasts in the pan and cook for 8–10 minutes on each side.

Meanwhile, place the soy sauce, peanut butter, lemon juice, water and a little pepper in a small saucepan. Mix well and heat gently, adjusting the consistency of the sauce with a little more water if necessary, so that it is slightly runny but coats the back of a spoon.

When the chicken is cooked, serve with the peanut sauce drizzled over the top, garnished with coriander and chopped fried peanuts, if liked. Serve with mixed vegetable noodles.

For egg fried rice, to serve as an alternative accompaniment, add 250 g (8 oz) long rice to a saucepan of boiling water. Simmer for 8 minutes, then add 150 g (5 oz) frozen peas and cook for 2 minutes before draining. Heat 1 teaspoon sunflower oil in a frying pan, add 2 beaten eggs and make a thin omelette. Roll the omelette up, shred and mix with the cooked rice.

miso chicken broth

Serves **4**

Preparation time **10 minutes**

Cooking time **16–18 minutes**

1 tablespoon **sunflower oil**

2 boneless, skinless **chicken breasts**, diced

250 g (8 oz) **cup mushrooms**, sliced

1 **carrot**, cut into thin matchsticks

1.5 cm (¾ inch) piece **root ginger**, grated

2 large pinches **dried crushed red chillies**

2 tablespoons **brown rice miso paste**

4 tablespoons **mirin** or **dry sherry**

2 tablespoons **light soy sauce**

1.2 litres (2 pints) **water**

2 **pak choi**, thinly sliced

4 **spring onions**, thinly sliced

4 tablespoons fresh chopped **coriander**

Heat the oil in a saucepan, add the chicken and fry for 4–5 minutes, stirring until golden. Add the mushrooms and carrot sticks, then the ginger, chillies, miso, mirin or sherry and soy sauce.

Pour on the water and bring to the boil, stirring. Simmer for 10 minutes.

Add the pak choi, spring onions and chopped coriander and cook for 2–3 minutes until the pak choi has just wilted. Spoon into bowls and serve.

For hot & sour chicken soup, fry the chicken in oil as above, add 125 g (4 oz) sliced mushrooms and 1 carrot, cut into matchsticks. Flavour with 2 finely chopped garlic cloves, 3 teaspoons red Thai curry paste, 1 tablespoon Thai fish sauce and 2 tablespoons light soy sauce. Add 1.2 litres (2 pints) chicken stock (see page 10), bring to the boil and cook for 10 minutes. Add 125 g (4 oz) sliced mini corn cobs, 50 g (2 oz) sliced mangetout, and spring onions and coriander as above. Cook for 2–3 minutes. Ladle into bowls and serve with lime wedges.

chicken tacos & hot green salsa

Serves **4**

Preparation time **10 minutes**

Cooking time **16–20 minutes**

1 tablespoon **sunflower oil**

4 x 175 g (6 oz) boneless,
   skinless **chicken breasts**

For the hot green salsa

1 **avocado**, chopped

1 **red onion**, finely chopped

1–2 **hot green** or **red chillies**,
   very finely chopped

1 **garlic clove**, very finely
   chopped

1 bunch **coriander**, roughly
   chopped

4 tablespoons **lime juice**

4 tablespoons **olive oil**

salt and **pepper**

To serve

16 **taco shells**

150 ml (¼ pint) **soured cream**

Heat a griddle pan (or ordinary frying pan). Brush the chicken breasts with sunflower oil, place them in the pan and cook for 8–10 minutes on each side. Remove from the pan and slice into strips.

To make the salsa, place the avocado in a bowl and add the onion, chillies, garlic and coriander. Mix together, adding the lime juice, olive oil and seasoning.

Pile some of the salsa in each of the taco shells and top with a few strips of chicken. Serve the remaining salsa separately, with a bowl of soured cream to spoon on top of the tacos just before eating.

For sweet potato jackets with chicken & tomato salsa, scrub and prick 4 medium-sized sweet potatoes then bake at 200°C (400°F), Gas Mark 6 for 50–60 minutes. Fry the chicken as above then dice. Make the salsa using 2 diced tomatoes in place of the avocado. Split the potatoes, top with spoonfuls of soured cream, chicken and salsa.

seared chicken & vegetable wraps

Serves **4**
Preparation time **5 minutes**
Cooking time **12–15 minutes**

4 boneless, skinless **chicken breasts**, cut into long thin slices
4 **courgettes**, cut into long thin slices
1 **red pepper**, cored, deseeded, quartered
1 **yellow pepper**, cored, deseeded, quartered
4 tablespoons **olive oil**
2 **garlic cloves**, finely chopped
4 teaspoons **sun-dried tomato paste**
4 large **soft flour tortillas**
200 g (7 oz) **cream cheese with garlic and herbs**
salt and **pepper**

Arrange the chicken breasts, courgettes and peppers in a single layer on a foil-lined grill rack or baking sheet.

Mix the oil, garlic, tomato paste and seasoning together and spoon over the chicken and vegetables. Grill for 12–15 minutes, turning once, until browned and the chicken is cooked through.

Warm the tortillas according to the instructions on the packet, then spread with the cream cheese. Cut the peppers into strips, peeling if liked. Divide the chicken and vegetables between the tortillas, then roll up tightly and cut in half. Serve warm.

For Chinese chicken wraps, grill the chicken drizzled with a mixture made from 2 tablespoons sunflower oil, 2 cloves finely chopped garlic, 2 teaspoons ordinary tomato paste and ¼ teaspoon ground Chinese 5-spice powder. Spread 6 tablespoons hoisin sauce over 4 warmed tortillas, then top with the chicken, 1 bunch of spring onions, cut into long thin strips, and ½ cucumber, deseeded and cut into long thin sticks. Roll up and halve as above.

chicken picnic terrine

Serves **8**
Preparation time **40 minutes**,
  plus chilling
Cooking time **1 hour**
  35 minutes

300 g (10 oz) **smoked
  streaky bacon**
1 tablespoon **olive oil**
1 **onion**, finely chopped
8 **Toulouse sausages**, about
  600 g (1 lb 2 oz), skins
  removed
125 g (4 oz) **chicken livers**,
  defrosted if frozen, diced
4 boneless, skinless **chicken
  thighs**, cut into small dice
1 **Granny Smith dessert
  apple**, cored, coarsely
  grated
¼ teaspoon **grated nutmeg**
50 g (2 oz) whole **pistachio
  nuts**
50 g (2 oz) **fresh
  breadcrumbs**
4 tablespoons **dry sherry** or
  brandy
salt and **pepper**

Use a strip of non-stick baking paper to line the base
and short sides of a 1 kg (2 lb) loaf tin. Stretch each
bacon rasher so it is half as long again, then butt close
together to line the tin. Cut rashers in half to line the
ends of the tin, and set aside a few rashers.

Heat the oil in a frying pan, add the onion and fry for
5 minutes until softened.

Mix the sausagemeat, chicken livers, chicken thighs,
apple, nutmeg, nuts, breadcrumbs and sherry or brandy
in a large bowl, then stir in the onions and seasoning.
Spoon the mixture into the bacon-lined tin, pressing it
down well.

Fold the ends of the bacon over the top, then cover
the gaps with the reserved rashers. Cover with foil,
stand the tin in a roasting tin and pour in hot water to
come halfway up the sides. Cook in a preheated oven,
180°C (350°F), Gas Mark 4, for 1½ hours or until
cooked when tested (see page 11).

Tip the water out of the roasting tin. Cool the terrine
then cover top of the loaf tin with weights and chill
overnight. Loosen the edges of the terrine, turn it out
of the tin and peel away the lining paper. Cut into thick
slices and serve with radishes.

For pickled walnut, apricot & chicken terrine,
use herb sausages and mix as above, replacing the
pistachios with 50 g (2 oz) drained and roughly
chopped pickled walnuts and 50 g (2 oz) chopped
ready-to-eat dried apricots. Finish as above.

chicken liver & pomegranate salad

Serves **4**

Preparation time **10 minutes**

Cooking time **8–9 minutes**

125 g (4 oz) **mixed salad leaves with baby red Swiss chard**

2 **Little Gem lettuces**, leaves separated

2 x 227 g (7½ oz) packs frozen **chicken livers**, just defrosted

50 g (2 oz) **butter**

2 tablespoons **olive oil**

1 **red onion**, sliced

2 **garlic cloves**, finely chopped

4 tablespoons **vodka** or **brandy**

½ **pomegranate**

salt and **pepper**

Rinse the salad leaves in a colander, then drain well and divide between 4 serving plates, tearing any large Little Gem leaves into bite-sized pieces.

Rinse the chicken livers in the colander, drain well, then roughly chop, discarding any white cores.

Heat the butter and oil in a large frying pan, add the onion and fry for 5 minutes until softened. Add the chicken livers and garlic and fry for 3–4 minutes until browned but still slightly pink in the centre.

Add the alcohol; as soon as it begins to bubble, light it with a long match, then stand back. As soon as the flames subside, season well, then spoon over the salad. Flex the pomegranate so that the seeds pop out, then sprinkle these over the salad and serve.

For chicken liver toasts, finely chop the onions and chicken livers, then fry as above. When cooked, spoon on to 12 slices of toasted French bread, and sprinkle with chopped parsley and a few chopped midget gherkins. Serve hot as an appetizer with drinks.

griddled chicken fajitas

Serves **4**
Preparation time **20 minutes**,
  plus marinating
Cooking time **16–20 minutes**

4 x 125 g (4 oz) boneless,
  skinless **chicken breasts**
4 large **soft flour tortillas**
150 ml (¼ pint) **soured cream**
4 **tomatoes**, skinned and
  sliced
1 **avocado**, sliced
4 **spring onions**, sliced
½ **red onion**, finely chopped
tortilla chips, to serve (optional)
salt and **pepper**

For the marinade
2 tablespoons **soy sauce**
3 cm (1¼ inch) piece **root
  ginger**, finely chopped
2 **garlic cloves**, finely
  chopped
2 tablespoons **olive oil**
1 bunch **fresh coriander**,
  chopped
1 **chilli**, chopped
2 tablespoons **lime juice**

Combine all the ingredients for the marinade in a
shallow dish. Add the chicken breasts and leave to
marinate at room temperature for 2 hours, or in the
refrigerator for 24 hours.

Heat a griddle pan (or ordinary frying pan). Place
the marinated chicken breasts in the pan to cook for
8–10 minutes on each side. When cooked, remove
the chicken from the pan and slice it into long strips.

Place the tortillas under a preheated grill and cook for
30 seconds on each side. Spread over one side of
each tortilla a spoonful of soured cream, a little tomato,
avocado and a sprinkling of spring onions and red onion.

Add the pieces of griddled chicken and season. Roll up
each tortilla tightly and cut in half across each one.
Serve with tortilla chips, if liked.

For guacamole, to accompany the fajitas, halve and
stone 2 ripe avocados. Scoop out the flesh then mash
with a fork. Mix with the juice of 1 lime, 3 tablespoons
chopped fresh coriander, 1 skinned and finely diced
tomato and if liked, 1 finely chopped jalapeno chilli.
Spoon on to the tortillas instead of soured cream.

chicken & vegetable skewers

Serves **4**

Preparation time **10 minutes**

Cooking time **15 minutes**

4 **chicken thighs**, skinned and boned

2 tablespoons **clear honey**

2 tablespoons **mild wholegrain mustard**

1 **courgette**, cut into 8 large pieces

1 **carrot**, cut into 8 large pieces

Cut the chicken thighs into bite-sized pieces and toss in the honey and mustard. Arrange the chicken pieces on a baking sheet and bake in a preheated oven, 180°C (350°F), Gas Mark 4, for 15 minutes until cooked through and lightly golden. Set aside and leave to cool.

Take 8 bamboo skewers and thread with the cooked chicken pieces and the raw vegetables.

Serve with the honey and mustard mixture for dipping. The skewers can also be refrigerated for adding to the following day's lunchbox.

For sticky chicken with honey & garlic, mix together 2 tablespoons tomato ketchup, 2 teaspoons runny honey, 2 finely chopped cloves of garlic and 1 tablespoon of sunflower oil. Dip the chicken into the ketchup mixture then cook as above. Thread on to skewers with 1 red pepper, deseeded, cored and cut into chunks and 8 cherry tomatoes.

chicken, tarragon & orange salad

Serves **4**
Preparation time **20 minutes**
Cooking time **45 minutes–
  1 hour**

1.5 kg (3 lb) **whole chicken**
1 medium **onion**, thinly sliced
grated rind and juice of
  1 orange
1 tablespoon chopped fresh
  tarragon (or 1 teaspoon
  dried)
1 **bay leaf**
1 tablespoon **olive oil**
½–1 tablespoon **white wine
  vinegar**
salt and **pepper**

To garnish
1 small **orange**, thinly sliced
small bunch **mustard and
  cress**
tarragon sprigs (optional)

Put the chicken, onion, orange rind and juice, tarragon and bay leaf in a large saucepan. Pour enough water over the top of the chicken to cover it and sprinkle with salt and pepper to taste. Cover, bring to the boil, and simmer for 1–1¼ hours, until the chicken is cooked.

Lift the chicken out of the saucepan and leave to cool. Discard the bay leaf and onion. Measure the stock, then boil until it reduces to 150 ml (½ pint). Set aside to cool, then chill in the refrigerator.

When the chicken is cold, take the meat off the bones, discarding the skin. Cut the meat into bite-sized pieces and place in a bowl.

When the stock has chilled, remove the layer of fat from the top, then reheat gently to thin it. Stir in the oil, add the vinegar, and season to taste. Pour this dressing over the chicken and toss well.

Serve immediately, garnished with orange slices, mustard, cress and tarragon sprigs, if liked, or cover and chill until required. The salad may also be served on a bed of shredded iceberg lettuce.

For chicken, tarragon & orange tagliatelle, add 150 ml (¼ pint) double cream to the cooled and reduced stock. Stir in the diced chicken then reheat. Add 25 g (1 oz) torn watercress and cook for 1 minute until the leaves just wilt. Toss with just-cooked tagliatelle.

chicken picnic loaf

Serves **12**
Preparation time **20 minutes**,
  plus marinating and chilling
Cooking time **20 minutes**

4 boneless, skinless **chicken
  breasts**, skinned
4 boneless **chicken thigh
  pieces**, skinned
1 tablespoon **lemon juice**
½ teaspoon **ground turmeric**
2 tablespoons **olive oil**
75 ml (3 fl oz) **water**
3 tablespoons chopped fresh
  mixed herbs
50 g (2 oz) **pistachio nuts**,
  toasted and roughly
  chopped
1 large round Eastern-style
  sesame loaf
250 g (8 oz) **chicken liver
  pâté**
salt and **pepper**

Rub the chicken pieces all over with the lemon juice, turmeric and half the oil, and season. Leave to marinate for 1 hour.

Heat the remaining oil in a frying pan and fry the chicken for 5 minutes until golden on both sides. Add the measured water, bring to the boil, then cover and simmer gently for 15 minutes. Leave to cool in the pan.

Remove the chicken and cut it into strips, reserving the pan juices. Place the chicken in a bowl and stir in the herbs, nuts and reserved juices.

Cut the top from the sesame loaf and scoop out the middle, leaving a 2.5 cm (1 inch) thick shell. (You could make breadcrumbs from the filling and freeze for later use if you like.)

Spoon half the chicken into the hollow bread and carefully spread the pâté over the top. Add the remaining chicken and replace the bread lid. Wrap the loaf tightly in clingfilm, weigh down with a heavy object and leave to chill overnight. Cut into wedges to serve.

For chicken & pistachio cous cous, marinade then fry the chicken as above. Mix with the herbs, nuts and reserved juices. Mix 2 teaspoons harissa paste with 450 ml (¾ pint) boiling water. Add 200 g (7 oz) cous cous and leave to soak for 5 minutes. Stir in the juice of ½ lemon, 2 chopped tomatoes and then the chicken and nut mix, before serving.

easy
suppers

chicken caldo verde

Serves **4**

Preparation time **20 minutes**

Cooking time **44–45 minutes**

2 tablespoons **olive oil**

1 **onion**, roughly chopped

125 g (4 oz) piece **chorizo**,
skinned, diced or sliced
depending on diameter

8 **chicken thighs**, boned,
skinned, cubed

500 g (1 lb) **baking potatoes**,
scrubbed, cubed

1 **garlic clove**, finely chopped

1 teaspoon **smoked paprika**

750 ml (1¼ pints) **chicken
stock** (see page 10)

400 g (13 oz) can **borlotti
beans**, drained

125 g (4 oz) **curly kale
leaves**

crusty bread, to serve

salt and **pepper**

Heat the oil in a large saucepan, add the onion and chorizo and fry for 5 minutes, stirring occasionally until the onion has softened. Add the chicken and fry for 5 more minutes until lightly browned.

Mix in the potatoes, garlic and paprika and cook for 1 minute, then add the stock, beans and a little salt and pepper. Bring to the boil, then cover and simmer for 30 minutes until the potatoes are tender.

Tear the kale into bite-sized pieces, add to the pan and push beneath the surface of the stock. Cook for 3–4 minutes until just wilted. Ladle into shallow bowls and serve with warm crusty bread.

For chicken caldo verde with pistou, replace the smoked paprika with 2 teaspoons pesto sauce, use haricot beans instead of borlotti beans, and use 125 g (4 oz) sliced green beans instead of the kale.

chicken with sage & lemon

Serves **4**
Preparation time **15 minutes**,
  plus marinating
Cooking time **20 minutes**

4 boneless, skinless **chicken
  breasts**, about 150 g
  (5 oz) each
5 tablespoons **olive oil**
3 tablespoons **lemon juice**
28 small **sage leaves**
3 tablespoons **unsalted
  butter**
cooked puy lentils, to serve
  (optional)
salt and **pepper**

Place the chicken breasts in a single layer in a
non-metallic dish. Pour over 3 tablespoons of the oil,
and the lemon juice. Scatter over the sage leaves, turn
the chicken so that the breasts are evenly coated, then
cover and leave to marinate for about 30 minutes.

Lift the chicken breasts from the marinade and reserve
the sage leaves separately. Pat the breasts dry. Strain
the marinade into a small bowl.

Heat the butter and the remaining oil in a frying pan,
add the chicken, and cook for about 10 minutes over a
moderate heat until browned. Turn the chicken breasts
over, season with salt and pepper, and tuck the sage
leaves around them. Cook for a further 10 minutes
until the underside is brown and the chicken is cooked
through. Transfer the chicken to a warmed serving
plate, cover and keep warm.

Tilt the pan and pour off the fat. Place the pan back on
the heat and stir in the reserved marinade, scraping up
any brown bits from the bottom of the pan. Boil until
reduced to a brown glaze. Serve the chicken in slices,
on a bed of puy lentils, if liked. Pour the remaining
marinade over the chicken and garnish with the
sage leaves.

For garlic & lemon mash, as an alternative to the
lentil accompaniment, boil 750 g (1 ½ lb) potatoes until
tender. Drain and mash with 50 g (2 oz) butter, the
grated rind and juice of ½ lemon and 3 cloves of finely
chopped garlic.

mojo chicken

Serves **4**
Preparation time **25 minutes**,
  plus marinating
Cooking time **10–12 minutes**

grated rind and juice of
  1 small **orange**
grated rind and juice of **1 lime**
1 tablespoon **sunflower oil**
1 large **mild red chilli**,
  deseeded, finely chopped
2 **garlic cloves**, finely
  chopped
2 teaspoons **light muscovado
  sugar**
1 teaspoon **cumin seeds**,
  roughly crushed
4 boneless, skinless **chicken
  breasts**, cubed
lemon wedges, to garnish

For the guacamole
2 ripe **avocados**
grated rind and juice of **1 lime**
small bunch **fresh coriander**,
  roughly snipped
salt and **pepper**

Mix the fruit rinds and juice, oil, chilli, garlic, sugar, cumin and a little seasoning together in a shallow china or glass dish. Add the chicken and toss together well. Cover with clingfilm, marinate in the refrigerator for 2 hours (or longer if you have time).

When ready to serve, thread the chicken on to 8 wooden or thin metal skewers. Cook under a hot grill, turning several times for 10–12 minutes until browned and cooked through.

Meanwhile, to make the guacamole, halve and stone the avocados and scoop the flesh out of the skin with a spoon. Roughly mash on a plate or in a food processor with the lime rind and juice. Season and stir in half the coriander.

Serve the skewers on plates garnished with the remaining coriander, lemon wedges, spoonfuls of guacamole and small bowls of salad and roasted sweet potatoes.

For citrus chicken wraps, cut the chicken into strips and marinate as above. Lift out of the marinade and fry in 1 tablespoon sunflower oil for 6–8 minutes until golden. Divide between 4 large soft flour tortillas, adding ½ crisp lettuce, finely shredded, 1 thinly sliced red onion and spoonfuls of the guacamole. Roll up tightly, then cut each one in half. Serve warm.

chicken cacciatore

Serves **4**
Preparation time **10 minutes**
Cooking time **20 minutes**

4 boneless, skinless **chicken breasts**, each about 125 g (4 oz)
500 g (1 lb) **cherry** or **mini plum tomatoes**, halved
1 **red onion**, cut into wedges
2 **garlic cloves**, finely chopped
2–3 stems **rosemary**, torn into pieces
6 tablespoons **red wine**
2 tablespoons **balsamic vinegar**
250 g (8 oz) **dried linguine** or **fettuccine**
2 tablespoons grated **fat-reduced mature Cheddar cheese** (optional)
pepper

Arrange the chicken in a large roasting tin or ovenproof dish so that it lies in a single layer. Add the tomatoes and onion, then sprinkle over the garlic and rosemary. Drizzle with the wine and vinegar and add a little pepper.

Bake in a preheated oven, 220°C (425°F), Gas Mark 7, for 20 minutes or until the onions and chicken are browned and the juices run clear when the chicken is pierced with a skewer.

Halfway through cooking, bring a large saucepan of water to the boil, add the pasta and cook for 8–10 minutes until just tender.

Drain the pasta and return to the empty pan. Slice the chicken breasts and add to the pasta with the onions, tomatoes and pan juices. Toss together and spoon into bowls. Sprinkle with a little rosemary and top with grated cheese, if liked.

For roast chicken & white bean salad, roast the chicken with the other ingredients as above, but rather than serving with pasta, mix with a 410 g (13½ oz) drained can of haricot or cannellini beans. Leave to cool then stir and toss with 40 g (1½ oz) mixed spinach, rocket and watercress salad.

chicken pimenton with puy lentils

Serves **4**

Preparation time **20 minutes**

Cooking time **20 minutes**

200 g (7 oz) **puy lentils**

3 tablespoons **olive oil**

6 **chicken thighs**, skinned, boned, cut into cubes

1 **red onion**, halved, sliced

1 tablespoon chopped **rosemary leaves**

¼ teaspoon **smoked paprika (pimenton)**

250 g (8 oz) **cherry tomatoes**, halved

2 tablespoons **balsamic vinegar**, plus a little extra

125 g (4 oz) **baby spinach leaves**, rinsed, drained

salt and **pepper**

Add the lentils to a saucepan of boiling water and simmer for 15–20 minutes until just tender. Meanwhile, heat 1 tablespoon of the oil in a large frying pan, add the chicken and onion and fry for 10 minutes, stirring until the chicken is browned.

Stir in the rosemary and paprika and cook for 1 minute, then mix in the tomatoes and seasoning and cook for 3–4 minutes, stirring until the tomatoes are just beginning to soften.

Drain the lentils into a sieve, add the remaining oil, vinegar and seasoning to the base of the dry pan and mix together. Return the lentils to the pan and mix in the spinach. Cook for 1 minute, stirring until the spinach is just beginning to wilt.

Spoon the lentil and spinach mixture on to serving plates and top with the chicken mix. Drizzle with a little extra balsamic vinegar, if liked. Serve immediately.

For creamy chicken rigatoni, omit the lentils. Cook the chicken and onion as above, adding paprika and rosemary. Add the spinach and when just wilted stir in 150 ml (¼ pint) double cream. Cook 375 g (12 oz) rigatoni pasta in boiling water until tender, then drain and stir into the cream mixture, heat through and serve in shallow bowls.

citrus chicken & fruited bulgar

Serves **4**
Preparation time **25 minutes**
Cooking time **12–17 minutes**

900 ml (1½ pints) **chicken stock** (see page 10)
¼ teaspoon **ground cinnamon**
¼ teaspoon **ground nutmeg** or **allspice**
250 g (8 oz) **bulgar wheat**
4 boneless, skinless **chicken breasts**, about 150 g (5 oz) each
grated rind of ½ **lemon**
grated rind of ½ **orange**
125 g (4 oz) ready-to-eat **dried apricots**
75 g (3 oz) stoned **dates**, chopped
75 g (3 oz) **sultanas**
juice of **1 orange**
small bunch **fresh coriander** or **basil**, torn, to garnish
salt and **pepper**

Pour the stock into the base of a steamer and add the ground spices and bulgar wheat.

Rinse the chicken breasts with cold water, drain them, then place in the steamer top and sprinkle with the lemon and orange rind and a little salt and pepper.

Bring the stock to the boil, put the steamer top in place, cover with a lid and cook for about 10 minutes until the chicken is thoroughly cooked and the bulgar is tender. Remove the steamer top and cook the bulgar for a few extra minutes if needed.

Stir the dried fruits and orange juice into the bulgar, then spoon the bulgar and any stock on to 4 plates. Slice the chicken pieces, arrange over the bulgar and garnish with torn herb leaves. Serve with a watercress and rocket salad.

For citrus chicken salad, steam the chicken with the fruit rinds and seasoning over a pan of simmering water. Cool then dice. Coarsely grate 2 carrots, peel and segment 2 oranges, slice 100 g (4 oz) fresh stoned dates. Arrange on a serving plate with the leaves torn from 1 Little Gem lettuce. Mix the juice of ½ lemon with 1 teaspoon caster sugar, 1 tablespoon orange flower water and a little salt. Drizzle this over the salad and garnish with torn coriander.

chicken arrabiata

Serves **4**
Preparation time **20 minutes**
Cooking time **36 minutes**

1 tablespoon **olive oil**
1 **onion**, roughly chopped
8 **chicken thighs**, boned,
  skinned, cut into cubes
2 **garlic cloves**, finely
  chopped
1 teaspoon **smoked paprika**
¼–½ teaspoon **dried crushed
  red chillies,** to taste
400 g (13 oz) can **chopped
  tomatoes**
250 ml (8 fl oz) **chicken stock**
  (see page 10)
375 g (12 oz) **macaroni**
large handful **rocket leaves,** to
  garnish
parmesan cheese, grated or
  shaved, to serve (optional)
salt and **pepper**

Heat the oil in a large saucepan, add the onion and fry for 5 minutes, stirring occasionally until softened. Add the chicken and fry for 5 more minutes until lightly browned.

Mix in the garlic, paprika and dried chillies and cook for 1 minute, then stir in the tomatoes, stock and a little salt and pepper. Bring to the boil, then cover and simmer for 25 minutes until the chicken is tender.

Meanwhile, half-fill a second pan with water, bring to the boil, then add the macaroni. Simmer for 10–12 minutes until just tender, then drain.

Stir the macaroni into the sauce and reheat if needed. Spoon into shallow bowls and garnish with the rocket leaves. Serve with grated or shaved Parmesan, if liked.

For chicken puttanesca, omit the chilli seeds and add 1 red pepper, cored, deseeded and diced, 2 teaspoons drained capers and 75 g (3 oz) marinated green and black olives. Toss with 375 g (12 oz) just-cooked spaghetti and sprinkle with grated Parmesan.

thai barbecued chicken

Serves **4–6**

Preparation time **20–25 minutes**, plus chilling time

Cooking time **30–40 minutes or 10–15 minutes**, depending on type of chicken

1.5 kg (3 lb) **whole chicken**, spatchcocked (see page 15), or part-boned **chicken breasts**

5 cm (2 inch) piece **galangal**, peeled, finely chopped

4 **garlic cloves**, crushed

1 large **red chilli**, finely chopped

4 **shallots**, finely chopped

2 tablespoons finely chopped **coriander leaves**

150 ml (¼ pint) **thick coconut milk**

chive flowers, to garnish

lime wedges, to serve

salt and **pepper**

Rub the chicken all over with salt and pepper and place in a shallow container.

Put the galangal, garlic, red chilli, shallots and coriander in a food processor and blend to a paste, or use a pestle and mortar. Add the coconut milk and mix until well blended. Pour over the chicken, cover and leave to marinate overnight in the refrigerator.

Remove the chicken from the marinade, place it on a hot barbecue and cook for 30–40 minutes for spatchcocked chicken and 10–15 minutes for chicken breasts, turning and basting regularly with the remaining marinade. The whole chicken is cooked when a skewer inserted in one of the legs reveals clear juices.

Leave the chicken to stand for 5 minutes, then chop it into small pieces with a cleaver. Garnish with chive flowers and eat with fingers. Serve with lime wedges, as well as a dipping sauce and sticky rice, if liked.

For sweet chilli sauce to serve as an accompaniment, wearing a pair of plastic gloves remove the seeds from 15 medium red chillies and finely chop the flesh. Place the chillies in a saucepan with 250 g (8 oz) granulated sugar, 150 ml (¼ pint) rice wine vinegar and 150 ml (¼ pint) water. Heat gently to dissolve the sugar, then increase the heat and simmer briskly for 20–25 minutes or until the liquid has reduced to a syrup. Pour the sauce into a sterilized glass jar or bottle and keep in the refrigerator until required.

catalan chicken

Serves **4**
Preparation time **15 minutes**
Cooking time **25 minutes**

2 tablespoons **olive oil**
40 g (1½ oz) **flaked almonds**
2 **onions**, roughly chopped
8 **chicken thighs**, boned,
   skinned, cubed
2 **garlic cloves**, finely
   chopped
100 g (3½ oz) **raisins**
200 ml (7 fl oz) **dry sherry**
250 ml (8 fl oz) **chicken stock**
   (see page 10)
small bunch **flat leaf parsley**,
   roughly chopped
salt and **pepper**

Heat a little of the oil in a large frying pan, add the almonds and fry, stirring for a few minutes until golden. Scoop out of the pan and set aside.

Add the remaining oil to the pan, then add the onions, chicken and garlic and fry over a medium heat for 10 minutes, stirring until deep golden. Mix in the raisins, sherry, stock and a little salt and pepper.

Simmer for 10 minutes until the sauce has reduced slightly and the chicken is cooked through. Sprinkle with the parsley and serve with rice and salad.

For Normandy chicken, omit the raisins and add 1 cored and diced Granny Smith dessert apple and 2 teaspoons Dijon mustard, replacing the sherry with 200 ml (7 fl oz) dry cider. Serve topped with spoonfuls of crème fraîche.

chicken skewers with couscous

Serves **4**

Preparation time **25 minutes**,
plus chilling time

Cooking time **20–25 minutes**

500 g (1 lb) boneless, skinless
chicken breasts

2 tablespoons **olive oil**

2 **garlic cloves**, crushed

½ teaspoon each **ground
cumin, turmeric, paprika**

2 teaspoons **lemon juice**

For the couscous

4 tablespoons **olive oil**

1 small **onion**, finely chopped

1 **garlic clove**, crushed

1 teaspoon each **ground
cumin, cinnamon, pepper,
ginger**

50 g (2 oz) **dried dates**

50 g (2 oz) **dried apricots**

50 g (2 oz) **blanched almonds**,
toasted

600 ml (1 pint) **vegetable
stock**, boiling

175 g (6 oz) **couscous**

1 tablespoon **lemon juice**

2 tablespoons chopped
coriander leaves

salt and **pepper**

Cut the chicken into long thin strips, place them in a
shallow dish and add the olive oil, garlic, spices and
lemon juice. Stir well, then cover and leave to marinate
for 2 hours. Thread the chicken strips on to 8 small,
presoaked wooden skewers.

Prepare the couscous by heating half the oil in a
saucepan and frying the onion, garlic and spices for
5 minutes. Chop and stir in the dried fruits and
almonds and remove from the heat.

Meanwhile, put the couscous in a heatproof bowl, add
the boiling stock and cover with a tea towel and steam
for 8–10 minutes, until the grains are fluffed up and
the liquid absorbed. Stir in the remaining oil and the
fruit and nut mixture, add the lemon juice and coriander
and season to taste.

While the couscous is steaming, griddle or grill the
chicken skewers for 4–5 minutes on each side, until
charred and cooked through. Serve with the couscous,
garnished with pomegranate seeds, lemon wedges and
coriander sprigs, if liked.

For roasted chicken with herb couscous, mix the
oil, garlic, spices and lemon juice and drizzle over
8 skinned and slashed chicken thighs. Roast at 190°C
(375°F) Gas Mark 5 for 35–45 minutes. Steam the
cous cous as above in stock. Stir in the remaining oil
and lemon juice. Add 4 finely chopped spring onions,
3 tablespoons chopped mint, 3 tablespoons chopped
parsley and 2 chopped tomatoes. Spoon on to plates,
top with the chicken and serve with lemon wedges.

speedy spiced chicken tagine

Serves **4**
Preparation time **20 minutes**
Cooking time **55 minutes**

1 tablespoon **olive oil**
8 **chicken thighs**, skinned
1 **onion**, sliced
2 **garlic cloves**, finely
  chopped
500 g (1 lb) **plum tomatoes**,
  skinned (optional), cut into
  chunks
1 teaspoon **turmeric**
1 **cinnamon stick**, halved
2.5 cm (1 inch) piece **root
  ginger**, grated
2 teaspoons **runny honey**
100 g (3½ oz) ready-to-eat
  dried apricots, quartered
200 g (7 oz) **couscous**
450 ml (¾ pint) **boiling water**
grated rind and juice of
  1 lemon
small bunch **fresh coriander**,
  roughly chopped
salt and **pepper**

Heat the oil in a large frying pan, add the chicken and fry until browned on both sides. Lift out and transfer to a tagine or casserole dish. Add the onion to the pan and fry until golden.

Stir in the garlic, tomatoes, spices and honey. Add the apricots and a little salt and pepper and heat through. Spoon over the chicken, cover the dish and bake in a preheated oven, 180°C (350°F), Gas Mark 4, for 45 minutes or until the chicken is cooked through.

When the chicken is almost ready, soak the couscous in boiling water for 5 minutes. Stir in the lemon rind and juice, coriander and seasoning. Spoon on to plates and top with the chicken and tomatoes, discarding the cinnamon stick just before eating.

For chicken & vegetable stew, use just 4 chicken thigh joints and add 1 diced carrot, 1 cored, deseeded and diced red pepper and 150 g (5 oz) frozen broad beans. Replace the cinnamon with 2 teaspoons harissa paste and add 150 ml (¼ pint) chicken stock (see page 10). Cook as above, adding 100 g (3½ oz) thickly sliced okra or green beans for the last 15 minutes of cooking. Sprinkle with chopped coriander or mint and serve with rice.

chicken with spinach & ricotta

Serves **4**
Preparation time **5 minutes**
Cooking time **25 minutes**

4 boneless, skinless **chicken breasts**, 125 g (4 oz) each
125 g (4 oz) **ricotta cheese**
125 g (4 oz) cooked **spinach**, squeezed dry
¼ teaspoon grated **nutmeg**
8 slices **Parma ham**
2 tablespoons **olive oil**, plus extra for drizzling
salt and **pepper**

To serve
lemon wedges
rocket leaves

Make a long horizontal slit through the thickest part of each chicken breast without cutting right through.

Crumble the ricotta into a bowl. Chop the spinach and mix into the ricotta with the nutmeg. Season with salt and pepper.

Divide the stuffing between the slits in the chicken breasts and wrap each one in 2 pieces of Parma ham, winding it around the chicken to cover the meat totally.

Heat the oil in a shallow ovenproof pan, add the chicken breasts and sauté for 4 minutes on each side or until the ham starts to brown. Transfer to a preheated oven, 200°C (400°F), Gas Mark 6, and cook for 15 minutes. Serve with lemon wedges and rocket leaves drizzled with olive oil.

For chicken with mozzarella & sun-dried tomatoes, instead of the ricotta, spinach and nutmeg, stuff each chicken breast with a thick slice of mozzarella and a sun-dried tomato piece, drained of its olive oil. Season well with black pepper and continue as in the main recipe.

chicken stew & dumplings

Serves **4**
Preparation time **30 minutes**
Cooking time **1 hour
  15 minutes**

8 boneless, skinless **chicken
  thighs**
1 tablespoons **sunflower oil**
1 **onion**, roughly chopped
2 **parsnips**, cut into chunks
2 **carrots**, cut into chunks
175 g (6 oz) **swede**, cut into
  chunks
50 g (2 oz) **pearl barley**
350 ml (12 fl oz) bottle
  pale ale
300 ml (½ pint) **chicken stock**
  (see page 10)
2 teaspoons made-up **English
  mustard**
salt and **pepper**

For the dumplings
175 g (6 oz) **self-raising flour**
75 g (3 oz) **light shredded
  suet**
4 tablespoons chopped **chives**
7–8 tablespoons **cold water**
salt and **pepper**

Cut each chicken thigh in half. Heat the oil in a flameproof casserole, add the chicken and onion and fry over a high heat until golden. Stir in the remaining vegetables and cook for 2 minutes, then mix in the barley, ale, stock and mustard. Season and bring to the boil. Cover and transfer to a preheated oven, 180°C (350°F), Gas Mark 4, for 1 hour.

When the chicken has finished cooking, make the dumplings by mixing the flour, suet, chives and some seasoning in a bowl. Stir in enough water to mix to a soft, slightly sticky dough, then shape dessertspoons of the mixture into balls.

Stir the chicken stew and transfer to the hob. When the stock is boiling, add the dumplings, cover and simmer for about 15 minutes or until the dumplings are light and fluffy. Spoon into shallow bowls to serve.

For chicken hotpot, omit the dumplings and cover the surface of the stew with 650 g (1¼ lb) thinly sliced potatoes before it goes into the oven. Cover and cook for 1 hour, remove the lid, dot with 25 g (1 oz) butter, season and cook for 30 minutes more until the potatoes are lightly browned.

lemon-infused chicken & spaghetti

Serves **4**

Preparation time **15 minutes**

Cooking time **16–20 minutes**

4 **lemons**

4 x 125 g (4 oz) boneless, skinless **chicken breasts**

1 bunch fresh **oregano**, chopped

300 g (10 oz) **spaghetti**

1 bunch fresh **parsley**, chopped

2 tablespoons **olive oil**

salt and **pepper**

Thinly slice 3 of the lemons, setting aside 8 large slices. Grate the rind and squeeze the juice from the fourth lemon, and set aside.

Using a sharp knife, make a pouch in the middle of each chicken breast. Fill each chicken pocket with the smaller slices of lemon, some chopped oregano leaves and salt and pepper.

Heat a griddle pan (or ordinary frying pan). Sandwich each chicken breast between 2 of the reserved large lemon slices and a sprig of oregano. Place the chicken in the pan and cook for 8–10 minutes on each side – try to keep the lemon intact with the chicken so that all the citrus flavour infuses into the chicken.

Meanwhile, bring a large saucepan of lightly salted water to the boil. When boiling, plunge the spaghetti into the water and cook for 12 minutes, or according to the instructions on the packet. Drain well, then toss with the lemon rind and juice, the parsley, the olive oil and seasoning to taste. Serve with the lemon chicken.

For lemon-infused chicken with rocket & lentil salad, omit the spaghetti and instead add 175 g (6 oz) puy lentils to a saucepan of boiling water. Simmer for 15–20 minutes or until tender. Cook the chicken with lemon slices and oregano as above. Add the remaining lemon juice, olive oil and seasoning to the cooked lentils then add 40 g (1½ oz) rocket leaves instead of the parsley. Serve with the chicken.

sticky mustard chicken & potatoes

Serves **4**

Preparation time **20 minutes**, plus standing

Cooking time **30 minutes**

2 tablespoons **sherry vinegar**
1 tablespoon **sunflower oil**
1 tablespoon **runny honey**
2 teaspoons **wholegrain mustard**
¼ teaspoon **turmeric**
4 boneless, skinless **chicken breasts**, each about 150 g (5 oz)
650 g (1 lb 6 oz) **new potatoes**
5 tablespoons **crème fraîche**
50 g (2 oz) **mixed spinach, rocket and watercress salad**, roughly chopped
salt and **pepper**

Mix the vinegar, oil, honey, mustard and turmeric in a shallow ovenproof dish with a little seasoning. Add the chicken and turn until completely coated. Leave to stand for 10 minutes.

Turn the chicken once more, then roast, still in the same dish, in a preheated oven, 200°C (400°F), Gas Mark 6, for 30 minutes until browned, spooning the glaze over halfway through cooking, and covering with foil if needed.

Meanwhile, cut any large potatoes in half and add to a saucepan of boiling water, then simmer for 15 minutes until tender. Drain and roughly crush with a fork, then mix with the crème fraîche, salad and seasoning, then warm through.

Test the chicken (see page 11). When it is cooked through, spoon the potatoes on to plates, then top with the chicken, spooning over any remaining glaze.

For sticky marmalade chicken, mix 2 tablespoons chunky marmalade with a 2.5 cm (1 inch) piece peeled and grated root ginger, 2 finely chopped garlic cloves, 1 teaspoon Dijon mustard, the juice of ½ orange and 1 tablespoon sunflower oil. Coat the chicken and bake as above. Serve with crushed new potatoes mixed with crème fraîche and 100 g (3½ oz) just-cooked frozen peas.

szechuan chicken

Serves **4**

Preparation time **5 minutes**, plus marinating

Cooking time **16–20 minutes**

3 tablespoons **soy sauce**

2 tablespoons **dry sherry**

1 teaspoon **rice vinegar**

3 cm (1¼ inch) piece **root ginger**, peeled and finely chopped

1 **garlic clove**, crushed

1 tablespoon **Chinese chilli paste**

½ teaspoon **Szechuan peppercorns**, ground

1 tablespoon **dark sesame oil**

4 x 125 g (4 oz) boneless, skinless **chicken breasts**

fresh coriander leaves, chopped, to garnish

Mix together all the ingredients except the chicken in a shallow dish to make the marinade. Add the chicken breasts, coat well with the marinade and leave to marinate at room temperature for 2 hours.

Heat a griddle pan (or ordinary frying pan). Cook the chicken for 8–10 minutes on each side and garnish with coriander. Serve with soba noodles and stir-fried oyster mushrooms.

For sesame greens with black bean sauce, to accompany the chicken, fry 2 tablespoons sesame seeds in 1 teaspoon sunflower oil until lightly browned. Add 1 tablespoon soy sauce, cover with a lid and take off the heat. When the bubbling subsides, scoop the seeds into a dish. Rinse 400 g (13 oz) spring greens and thickly slice, stir fry in 1 tablespoon oil with 2 cloves finely chopped garlic until just wilted. Mix in 3 tablespoons ready-made black bean sauce. Serve sprinkled with the seeds.

polenta crusted chicken strips

Serves **4**

Preparation time **20 minutes**

Cooking time **15 minutes**

250 g (8 oz) **instant polenta grains**

8 tablespoons ready-grated **Parmesan cheese**

2 **eggs**

4 boneless, skinless **chicken breasts**, cut into slices of even thickness

50 g (2 oz) **sun-dried tomatoes in oil**, sliced

300 g (10 oz) **cherry tomatoes**, halved

3 tablespoons **olive oil**

2 teaspoons **green pesto**

800 ml (1 pint 7 fl oz) **water**

125 ml (4 fl oz) **double cream**

tiny **basil leaves**, to garnish (optional)

salt and **pepper**

Mix 50 g (2 oz) polenta on a plate with 2 tablespoons of Parmesan. Beat the eggs in a shallow dish. Dip the chicken slices into the egg, then roll in the polenta mix until thinly coated. Put on a plate and set aside.

Put the sun-dried tomatoes into a shallow ovenproof dish, then put the fresh tomatoes on top, add 1 tablespoon oil, the pesto and a little seasoning. Grill for 5 minutes.

Bring the measured water to the boil in a nonstick saucepan, add the remaining polenta, bring back to the boil and stir constantly until thickened and smooth. Mix in the remaining Parmesan and season generously. Set aside.

Heat the remaining oil in a frying pan, add the chicken and fry for 8–10 minutes, turning until golden and cooked through. Reheat the soft polenta, gradually mixing in the cream and a little extra water if needed, until soft.

Spoon the polenta on to plates, top with the tomatoes, then arrange the chicken strips on top. Garnish with basil leaves, if liked.

For chicken strips with garlicky tomato sauce, make up the chicken as above but coating in 100 g (3½ oz) fresh breadcrumbs mixed with 2 tablespoons Parmesan instead of the polenta. Cook as above. Meanwhile, fry 1 chopped onion in 1 tablespoon olive oil until softened. Add 2 finely chopped garlic cloves, a 400 g (13 oz) can chopped tomatoes, 1 teaspoon caster sugar and seasoning. Simmer for 5 minutes. Serve with the chicken and chunky oven chips.

oriental chicken cakes

Serves **4**

Preparation time **15 minutes**

Cooking time **16 minutes**

575 g (1 lb 3 oz) **minced chicken**

1 stalk **lemon grass**, very finely chopped

2 **kaffir lime leaves**, very finely chopped

5 cm (2 inch) piece **root ginger**, peeled, very finely chopped

2 **green chillies**, very finely chopped

2 **garlic cloves**, very finely chopped

1 **egg**, beaten

1 tablespoon **sesame seeds**, toasted

chilli and ginger jam (see page 174), to serve

Place the chicken in a large bowl with the lemon grass, kaffir lime leaves, ginger, chilli and garlic, which need to be so finely chopped as to almost make a paste. Add the beaten egg and sesame seeds. Mix well, using your hands.

Heat a griddle pan (or ordinary frying pan). Divide the mixture into 24 and shape into small patties. Cook for 8 minutes on each side.

Serve the chicken cakes with chilli and ginger jam (see page 174), a salad of rice noodles, chopped peanuts, sliced onion, beansprouts and lots of chopped coriander.

For Chinese leaf & beansprout salad, as an alternative salad accompaniment, mix 4 tablespoons sunflower oil, 2 tablespoons rice vinegar, 2 tablespoons light soy sauce and 2 teaspoons fish sauce in a bowl. Add 400 g (13 oz) sliced Chinese leaves, 100 g (3½ oz) rinsed and drained beansprouts, 4 sliced spring onions, 250 g (8 oz) carrots cut into matchstick strips, 50 g (2 oz) roughly chopped salted peanuts and 2 tablespoons chopped mint then toss together.

thai chicken satay

Serves **4**

Preparation time **30 minutes**,
   plus marinating

Cooking time **16 minutes**

4 boneless, skinless **chicken
   breasts,** cut into thin slices
2 **garlic cloves,** finely chopped
4 cm (1½ inch) piece **root
   ginger,** peeled and grated
2 tablespoons **light soy sauce**
2 tablespoons **lemon juice**
1 tablespoon **sunflower oil**
2 **shallots** or ½ **onion,**
   finely sliced
1 **garlic clove,** finely sliced
1 small hot **Thai chilli,**
   thinly sliced
2.5 cm (1 inch) piece **root
   ginger,** peeled and grated
4 tablespoons **crunchy
   peanut butter**
200 ml (7 fl oz) canned **low-
   fat coconut milk**
2 teaspoons **fish sauce**
1 tablespoon **light soy sauce**

Mix the chicken with the garlic, ginger, light soy sauce and lemon juice and then leave to stand for 30 minutes.

Heat the sunflower oil in a small saucepan. Add the shallots or onion and fry gently until softened but not brown. Mix in the garlic, chilli and second batch of ginger and cook for 1 minute before adding all the remaining ingredients. Simmer gently for 5 minutes.

Thread the marinaded chicken slices in a zigzag pattern on to 12 thin metal skewers. Cook under a hot grill for 10 minutes, turning once or twice until the chicken is browned and cooked through. Garnish with lime wedges and serve with rice and a salad.

For pickled Thai cucumber salad, to serve with the chicken satay, heat 4 tablespoons rice vinegar in a saucepan with 4 tablespoons caster sugar and ½–1 thinly sliced hot Thai red chilli to taste. When the sugar has dissolved, boil for 1 minute. Add ½ a thinly sliced cucumber and leave to cool.

oriental 5-spice glazed chicken

Serves **4**

Preparation time **20 minutes**

Cooking time **40–45 minutes**

2 **red onions**, cut into wedges

2 tablespoon **sunflower oil**

4 **chicken thighs**

4 **chicken drumsticks**

4 **red plums**, halved, stoned

3 tablespoons **redcurrant jelly**

1 tablespoon **red wine vinegar**

2 tablespoons **dark soy sauce**

½ teaspoon **5-spice powder**

150 ml (¼ pint) **water**

100 g (3½ oz) **pak choi**

Toss the onion wedges in 1 tablespoon of the oil in a large roasting tin. Slash each chicken joint 2–3 times with a knife, then add to the roasting tin with the plums.

Warm the redcurrant jelly, vinegar, soy sauce and 5-spice in a small saucepan until the jelly has melted, then brush liberally over the chicken, reserving about one-third for later. Pour the measured water into the base of the tin, avoiding the chicken, so that the glaze will not burn on the bottom of the tin.

Roast, uncovered in a preheated oven, 190°C (375°F), Gas Mark 5, for 40–45 minutes, brushing with the remaining glaze once during cooking. Test the chicken (see page 11).

Heat the remaining oil in a frying pan and add the pak choi. Fry for 2–3 minutes until tender and then add to the roasting tin just before serving.

Spoon on to plates and serve with rice.

For balsamic glazed chicken, toss the onions in 1 tablespoon olive oil, then add the chicken as above but with 275 g (9 oz) Chantenay carrots instead of the plums. Mix 3 tablespoons balsamic vinegar with 3 tablespoons white wine, 1 tablespoon olive oil and 1 tablespoon runny honey, then brush this over the chicken in place of the redcurrant glaze, tucking 4 bay leaves in between the joints. Roast as above with the water.

griddled chicken burgers

Serves **4**

Preparation time **20 minutes**

Cooking time **12–20 minutes**

625 g (1¼ lb) **minced chicken**

1 **shallot**, finely chopped

1 small bunch **thyme**, chopped, plus extra to garnish (optional)

1 teaspoon **Worcestershire sauce**

3 drops **Tabasco sauce**

2 **egg yolks**

1 **ciabatta loaf**

Dijon mustard, for spreading

mayonnaise, for spreading

2 **tomatoes**, sliced

1 bag **herb salad leaves**

salt and **pepper**

Place the chicken in a large bowl. Add the shallot, thyme, Worcestershire and Tabasco sauces and egg yolks. Season to taste and mix well.

Heat a griddle pan (or ordinary frying pan). Using your hands, divide the chicken mixture into 4. Shape into patties and cook for 6–10 minutes on each side, depending on the thickness of the patties.

Cut the ciabatta in half horizontally and toast the 2 lengths under a preheated grill. Cut each piece in half. Spread the ciabatta with mustard and mayonnaise. Top with tomato slices and herb salad leaves, finally adding the griddled chicken burgers on top. Garnish with a little chopped thyme, if liked.

For Mediterranean burgers, omit the Worcestershire sauce and stir in 50 g (2 oz) each of pitted and chopped black olives and sundried tomatoes, drained of their oil. Shape, cook and serve as above, minus the mustard.

creamy chicken gnocchi

Serves **4**

Preparation time **15 minutes**

Cooking time **14–16 minutes**

2 tablespoons **olive oil**

1 **onion**, thinly sliced

500 g (1 lb) **butternut squash**, peeled, deseeded, cut into small dice

4 rashers **smoked streaky bacon**, diced

450 g (14 oz) **mini chicken breast fillets**, diced

12 **sage leaves**

300 ml (½ pint) **chicken stock** (see page 10)

500 g (1 lb) pack **chilled gnocchi**

6 tablespoons **crème fraîche**

4 tablespoons freshly grated **Parmesan cheese**

salt and **pepper**

Heat the oil in a frying pan, add the onion, butternut squash and bacon and fry for 5 minutes until just beginning to brown. Stir in the chicken and sage and fry for 5 minutes, stirring until golden.

Add the stock and a little seasoning and cook for 2–3 minutes until the chicken and squash are cooked through.

Bring a large saucepan of water to the boil, add the gnocchi and cook for 2–3 minutes until the gnocchi rise to the surface. Drain and add to the frying pan with the crème fraîche. Gently toss together, then spoon into shallow bowls and sprinkle with the Parmesan.

For chicken, butternut squash & sage risotto, mix 200 g (7 oz) risotto rice into the fried-chicken mixture, then stir in 150 ml (¼ pint) dry white wine and 1 litre (1¾ pints) hot chicken stock (see page 10), in three batches, topping up as the rice absorbs the liquid. Simmer uncovered for 20 minutes, stirring occasionally until the rice is soft. Spoon into bowls and sprinkle with Parmesan.

blackened chicken & beans

Serves **4**
Preparation time **30 minutes**
Cooking time **40 minutes**

4 **chicken thighs**
4 **chicken drumsticks**
1 teaspoon **cumin seeds**
1 teaspoon **fennel seeds**
1 teaspoon **dried thyme
leaves**
¼ teaspoon **ground cinnamon**
½ teaspoon **smoked paprika**
1 tablespoon **sunflower oil**
1 tablespoon **tomato purée**
1 tablespoon **vinegar**
2 tablespoons **dark
muscovado sugar**
2 tablespoons **pineapple
juice** (from can below)

For the black-eye bean salad
227 g (7½ oz) can **pineapple
in juice**, juice reserved,
pineapple chopped
410 g (13½ oz) can **black-eye
beans**, drained
small bunch **fresh coriander**,
roughly chopped
½ **red onion**, finely chopped
1 **red pepper**, cored,
deseeded, diced
grated rind and juice of **1 lime**

Slash the chicken joints 2–3 times with a knife, then put into a roasting tin. Roughly crush the seeds then mix with the next 8 ingredients together and spoon over the chicken.

Add 4 tablespoons water to the base of the roasting tin, then bake the chicken in a preheated oven, 180°C (350°F), Gas Mark 4, for 40 minutes, spooning pan juices over once or twice until the chicken is deep brown in colour and the juices run clear when the chicken is tested (see page 11).

Meanwhile, to make the bean salad, pour the remaining canned pineapple juice into a bowl and add the chopped pineapple and all the remaining ingredients. Mix together, then serve spoonfuls with the cooked chicken.

For blackened chicken with rice & peas, bake the chicken as above but omit the black-eye bean salad. Bring 1 litre (1¾ pints) chicken stock (see page 10) and a 400 ml (14 fl oz) can low-fat coconut milk to the boil in a saucepan. Add 200 g (7 oz) long-grain white rice that has been rinsed with cold water and drained, and a 410 g (13½ oz) can drained red kidney beans. Simmer for 8 minutes, add 125 g (4 oz) frozen peas and top up with extra boiling water. Cook for 2 minutes, then serve with the chicken.

thai sesame chicken patties

Serves **4**

Preparation time **15 minutes**, plus chilling

Cooking time **10 minutes**

4 **spring onions**

15 g (½ oz) **fresh coriander**, plus extra to garnish

500 g (1 lb) **minced chicken**

3 tablespoons **sesame seeds**, toasted

1 tablespoon **light soy sauce**

3.5 cm (1½ inch) piece **root ginger**, finely grated

1 **egg white**

1 tablespoon **sesame oil**

1 tablespoon **sunflower oil**

Thai sweet chilli dipping sauce, to serve

spring onion curls, to garnish (optional)

Finely chop the spring onions and coriander in a food processor or with a knife. Mix with the chicken, sesame seeds, soy sauce, ginger and egg white.

Divide the mixture into 20 mounds on a chopping board, then shape into slightly flattened rounds with wetted hands. Chill for 1 hour (or longer if you have time).

Heat the sesame and sunflower oils in a large frying pan, add the patties and fry for 10 minutes, turning once or twice until golden and cooked through to the centre. Arrange on a serving plate with a small bowl of chilli dipping sauce in the centre. Garnish with extra coriander leaves and spring onion curls, if liked.

For baby leaf stir-fry with chilli to serve as an accompaniment, heat 2 teaspoons sesame oil in the finished pattie pan, add a 250 g (8 oz) pack of ready-prepared baby leaf and baby vegetable stir-fry ingredients and stir-fry for 2–3 minutes until the vegetables are hot. Mix in 2 tablespoons light soy sauce and 1 tablespoon Thai sweet chilli dipping sauce. Serve in a side bowl with the chicken patties.

stoved chicken with black pudding

Serves **4**

Preparation time **20 minutes**

Cooking time **2 hours 5 minutes**

4 **chicken thigh** and **drumstick joints**

2 tablespoons **plain flour**

1 tablespoon **sunflower oil**

2 **onions**, thinly sliced

50 g (2 oz) **butter**

1 kg (2 lb) **potatoes**, thinly sliced

1 **dessert apple**, cored, diced

125 g (4 oz) **black pudding**, peeled, diced

450 ml (¾ pint) **chicken stock** (see page 10)

salt and **pepper**

Coat the chicken in the flour and seasoning.

Heat the oil in a large frying pan, add the onions and fry for 5 minutes until pale golden. Mix in any remaining flour, then scoop the onions out of the pan and set aside.

Heat half the butter in the frying pan, add the chicken and fry on both sides until golden. Arrange a thin layer of potatoes in the base of an ovenproof casserole dish, top with half the onions, then the chicken pieces. Add the apple and black pudding, then spoon over the remaining onions. Arrange the remaining potatoes in an overlapping layer on the top. Pour the stock over the top, then season the potatoes.

Cover the dish tightly and cook in a preheated oven, 180°C (350°F), Gas Mark 4, for 1½ hours. Remove the lid, dot the potatoes with the remaining butter and cook for 30 minutes more until golden brown. Serve in shallow bowls.

For stoved chicken with bacon & sage, omit the black pudding and apple and add 125 g (4 oz) diced smoked streaky bacon when frying the onions. Add 2–3 stems sage, depending on size, to the casserole dish along with the fried chicken.

italian pesto chicken burgers

Serves **4**

Preparation time **15 minutes**,
   plus chilling

Cooking time **10–13 minutes**

500 g (1 lb) **minced chicken**

2 **garlic cloves**, finely
   chopped

4 **spring onions**, finely
   chopped

2 teaspoons **pesto**

1 **egg yolk**

1 tablespoon **sunflower oil**

4 **ciabatta rolls**

2 tablespoons **mayonnaise**

40 g (1½ oz) **rocket,
   watercress and spinach
   salad**

50 g (2 oz) **sun-dried
   tomatoes in oil**, drained,
   sliced

salt and **pepper**

Put the chicken, garlic, spring onions, pesto and
egg yolk in a bowl, add seasoning, then mix together
well. Divide into 4, then shape into thick burgers. Chill
for 1 hour.

Heat the oil in a nonstick frying pan, add the burgers
and fry for about 10–13 minutes, turning once or twice
until golden brown and cooked through.

Split the ciabatta rolls in half and lightly toast the cut
sides. Spread with mayonnaise, then add the salad and
tomatoes to the lower half of each roll. Top with the
burgers and the other half of each roll, and serve with
oven chips.

For curried chicken burgers, mix 2 teaspoons hot
curry paste and 2 tablespoons chopped coriander into
the chicken mixture instead of the pesto. Fry as above,
then serve in warmed round naan breads with salad
and mango chutney.

chicken tikka masala

Serves **4**
Preparation time **20 minutes**
Cooking time **20 minutes**

25 g (1 oz) **butter**
4 boneless, skinless **chicken breasts**, cubed
1 **onion**, quartered
3.5 cm (1½ inch) piece **root ginger**, sliced
3 **garlic cloves**, sliced
1 **hot red chilli**, sliced, including seeds
1 teaspoon **cumin seeds**, roughly crushed
1 teaspoon **coriander seeds**, roughly crushed
1 teaspoon **turmeric**
1 teaspoon **paprika**
2 teaspoons **garam masala**
300 ml (½ pint) **chicken stock** (see page 10)
150 ml (¼ pint) **double cream**
4 tablespoons **fresh coriander**, chopped, plus extra to garnish
juice of ½–1 lemon

Heat the butter in a saucepan, add the chicken and fry for 3 minutes. Finely chop the onion, ginger, garlic and chilli in a food processor or with a knife. Add to the chicken and fry for 5 minutes, stirring until lightly browned.

Mix in the spices and cook for 3–4 minutes until well coloured. Stir in the stock and cream, then simmer for 10 minutes, stirring occasionally until the chicken is tender.

Stir in the chopped coriander and lemon juice to taste. Cook for 1 minute, then garnish with extra coriander. Serve with rice and naan bread.

For chicken tikka, mix the diced chicken breast with the juice of ½ lemon and ¼ teaspoon salt. Mix 150 g (5 fl oz) natural yogurt with 3.5 cm (1½ inch) grated root ginger, 3 finely chopped garlic cloves, and 1 finely chopped red chilli. Stir in the spices as above and add 4 tablespoons sunflower oil. Marinate in the refrigerator overnight. Spoon the chicken on to a foil-lined baking sheet and cook in a preheated oven, 220°C (425°F), Gas Mark 7, for 15 minutes, turning the chicken and brushing with the remaining marinade halfway through cooking. Serve with salad.

chicken balti with whole spices

Serves **4**
Preparation time **20 minutes**
Cooking time **38–41 minutes**

1 **onion**, quartered
2.5 cm (1 inch) piece **root ginger**, sliced
3 **garlic cloves**
2 tablespoons **sunflower oil**
8 boneless, skinless **chicken thighs**, cut into cubes
1 teaspoon **cumin seeds**, roughly crushed
1 **cinnamon stick**, halved
8 **cardamom pods**, roughly crushed
6 **cloves**
½ teaspoon **turmeric**
1 teaspoon **dried crushed red chillies**
400 g (13 oz) can **chopped tomatoes**
600 ml (1 pint) **chicken stock** (see page 10)
small bunch **fresh coriander**
25 g (1 oz) **flaked almonds**, toasted, to garnish

Finely chop the onion, ginger and garlic in a food processor or with a large knife. Heat the oil in a medium saucepan, add the chicken and fry for 5 minutes, stirring until lightly browned. Stir in the chopped onion mix and fry for 2–3 minutes until softened.

Stir in the spices and chillies and cook for 1 minute, then mix in the tomatoes and stock. Bring to the boil, then cover and simmer for 30 minutes, stirring occasionally.

Tear the coriander into pieces, add to the balti and cook for 1 minute, then spoon into bowls. Garnishing with the toasted almonds, serve with rice and naan bread.

For chicken balti with mushrooms & spinach, omit the seeds, cardamom, cloves, turmeric and dried chillies and stir in 2 tablespoons medium hot balti curry paste instead. Mix in 125 g (4 oz) sliced cup mushrooms and cook as above. Stir in 150 g (5 oz) baby leaf spinach along with the coriander at the end and cook until the spinach has just wilted.

maple glazed chicken

Serves **4**
Preparation time **15 minutes**
Cooking time **40–45 minutes**

4 **chicken thigh** and
   drumstick joints
2 **dessert apples**, cored,
   quartered
250 g (8 oz) **shallots**, peeled,
   halved if large
625 g (1¼ lb) **parsnips**,
   quartered
6 **bay leaves**
2 tablespoons **olive oil**
2 tablespoons **maple syrup**
2 tablespoons **cider vinegar**
salt and **pepper**

Slash the chicken joints 3–4 times, then put them into a large roasting tin with the apples, shallots, parsnips and bay leaves.

Mix the remaining ingredients together and spoon over the chicken and vegetables. Add 4 tablespoons water to the base of the tin. Cook in a preheated oven, 190°C (375°F), Gas Mark 5, for 40–45 minutes, spooning the glaze over the chicken once or twice until deep brown and cooked through when tested (see page 11).

Spoon on to plates and serve with a rocket salad.

For mango chutney-glazed chicken, add 1 small mango, peeled, stoned and cut into thick slices instead of the apple. Omit the maple syrup and mix 2 tablespoons mango chutney with the oil and vinegar mix. Cook as above. Mix 150 g (5 oz) natural yogurt with 3 tablespoons fresh chopped coriander and an extra tablespoon of mango chutney. Serve spoonfuls with the chicken.

chicken, bacon & sage meatballs

Serves **4**

Preparation time **30 minutes**, plus chilling

Cooking time **20 minutes**

125 g (4 oz) **cup mushrooms**, finely chopped

2 rashers **smoked streaky bacon**, chopped

500 g (1 lb) **minced chicken**

2 tablespoons **fresh sage**, finely chopped

1 **egg yolk**

2 tablespoons **sunflower oil**

2 **onions**, thinly sliced

2 teaspoons **caster sugar**

2 tablespoons **plain flour**

450 ml (¾ pint) **chicken stock** (see page 10)

salt and **pepper**

Mix the mushrooms and bacon with the chicken, then stir in the sage, egg yolk and seasoning. Shape into 20 small meatballs and chill for 30 minutes.

Fry the meatballs in 1 tablespoon of the oil for 5 minutes until lightly browned all over, then transfer to a roasting tin and cook in a preheated oven, 190°C (375°F), Gas Mark 5, for 15 minutes.

Meanwhile, fry the onions in the remaining oil in the cleaned frying pan until softened and just beginning to brown. Sprinkle over the sugar and cook for 5 minutes more, stirring frequently until a deep brown.

Mix in the flour, then gradually mix in the stock, season and bring to the boil. Simmer for 2–3 minutes until thickened. Add the meatballs to the gravy and gently stir. Spoon into bowls and serve with mashed potatoes, peas and green beans.

For chicken meatballs with mustard sauce, oven-bake the meatballs as above. Wash and dry the frying pan, then fry 1 chopped onion in 50 g (2 oz) butter until softened but not browned. Stir in 40 g (1½ oz) plain flour, then gradually mix in 450 ml (¾ pints) chicken stock (see page 10). Stir in 3 teaspoons mild Dijon or Swedish mustard, ½ teaspoon turmeric and seasoning. Simmer and finish as above.

chicken thatch

Serves **4**

Preparation time **25 minutes**

Cooking time **35 minutes**

1 tablespoon **sunflower oil**

4 boneless, skinless **chicken thighs**, diced

1 **onion**, chopped

2 tablespoons **plain flour**

450 ml (¾ pint) **chicken stock** (see page 10)

2 teaspoons **Dijon mustard**

1 large **carrot**, diced

750 g (1½ lb) **potatoes**, quartered

150 g (5 oz) **courgettes**, diced

75 g (3 oz) **sugar snap peas**, halved

75 g (3 oz) **frozen peas**

40 g (1½ oz) **butter**

3 tablespoons **milk**

75 g (3 oz) **mature Cheddar cheese**, grated

salt and **pepper**

Heat the oil in a saucepan, add the chicken and onion and fry for 5 minutes, stirring until browned. Stir in the flour, then gradually mix in the stock. Bring to the boil, then add the mustard, carrot and a little seasoning. Cover and simmer for 30 minutes.

Meanwhile, cook the potatoes in a saucepan of boiling water until tender. Add the courgettes, sugar snap peas and frozen peas to a smaller saucepan of boiling water and cook for 3 minutes. Drain and set aside.

Drain the potatoes and mash with two-thirds of the butter and all the milk. Season and stir in two-thirds of the cheese.

Spoon the chicken mixture into a 1.3 litre (2¼ pint) pie dish or 4 individual dishes, add the just-cooked green vegetables, then spoon the mash on top. Dot with the remaining butter and sprinkle with the remaining cheese. Grill until golden, then serve immediately. (For an oven-baked chicken thatch, chill the dish once the grated cheese has been sprinkled on top, then bake when needed, in a preheated oven, 190°C (375°F), Gas Mark 5, for 35 minutes until piping hot or 25 minutes for smaller dishes.)

For chicken & bacon thatch, add 4 chopped rashers of smoked back bacon when frying the chicken and onion. Omit the courgettes, sugar snaps and peas and cook 125 g (4 oz) frozen sweetcorn instead. Drain and add to the chicken. Finish as above.

chicken liver & pancetta ragu

Serves **4**
Preparation time **15 minutes**
Cooking time **16–17 minutes**

400 g (13 oz) **tagliatelle**
1 tablespoon **olive oil**
4 boneless, skinless **chicken
  thighs**, diced
1 **onion**, chopped
75 g (3 oz) **pancetta**, diced
125 g (4 oz) **chicken livers**,
  defrosted if frozen, well rinsed
2 **garlic cloves**, finely chopped
150 ml (¼ pint) **red wine**
125 ml (4 fl oz) **chicken stock**
  (see page 10)
4 teaspoons **sun-dried
  tomato paste**
small bunch **basil**
Parmesan cheese, grated, to
  garnish
salt and **pepper**

Bring a large saucepan of water to the boil, add the
tagliatelle and cook for 8–10 minutes until just tender,
then drain into a colander.

Meanwhile, heat the oil in a large frying pan, add the
chicken, onion and pancetta and fry for 10 minutes,
stirring until golden. Chop the chicken livers, discarding
any white cores, then add to the pan with the garlic
and fry for 3 minutes.

Stir in the red wine, stock and tomato paste, then a
little seasoning. Cook over a high heat for 3–4 minutes
until the sauce is reduced slightly. Tear half the basil
leaves into pieces and add to the chicken, then cook
for 1 minute.

Stir the tagliatelle into the chicken mixture and reheat
if needed. Spoon into shallow bowls and sprinkle with
the remaining basil leaves and grated Parmesan.

For chicken & walnut ragu, omit the chicken livers
and use 50 g (2 oz) roughly chopped walnut pieces
instead. Toss with chopped parsley and sprinkle with
extra parsley to garnish.

chicken maryland & banana fritters

Serves **4**

Preparation time **25 minutes**

Cooking time **20 minutes**

50 g (2 oz) **plain flour**

¼ teaspoon each **dry mustard powder, turmeric** and **cayenne pepper**

8 **chicken drumsticks**

4 tablespoons **milk**

4 tablespoons **sunflower oil**

200 g (7 oz) **frozen sweetcorn**

4 tablespoons **double cream**

4 tablespoons **water**

4 **spring onions**, chopped

1 **red pepper**, cored, deseeded, diced

parsley, chopped, to garnish (optional)

salt

For the banana fritters

1 small ripe **banana**

125 g (4 oz) **self-raising flour**

2 **eggs**

½ teaspoon **dried crushed red chillies**

150 ml (¼ pint) **milk**

salt and **pepper**

Mix the flour, mustard, turmeric, cayenne and a pinch of salt on a plate. Dip the chicken in the milk, then coat thickly in the flour and spice mixture.

Heat 3 tablespoons of the oil in a frying pan, add the chicken and fry, turning, until golden all over. Transfer to a roasting tin and cook in a preheated oven, 200°C (400°F), Gas Mark 6, for 20 minutes or until the chicken is cooked through when tested (see page 11).

Meanwhile, put the sweetcorn, cream, water, spring onions and red pepper into a saucepan, cover and simmer for 5 minutes until hot, then set aside.

Make the fritters by mashing the banana on a plate, then putting it into a bowl with the flour, eggs, chillies and seasoning. Gradually whisk in the milk until smooth. Heat the remaining oil in the cleaned frying pan, add dessertspoonfuls of the fritter mixture and fry over a moderate heat until bubbles appear on the surface and the undersides are golden. Turn over and cook the second side until golden. Keep hot.

Reheat the corn mixture, then spoon into small bowls set on dinner plates, add the chicken and fritters to the plates and garnish with chopped parsley, if liked.

For chicken Maryland with fried bananas & bacon,

bake the chicken as above. Simmer 4 halved corn cobs in a pan of water for 15 minutes until tender. Wash and dry the chicken pan, then fry 2 thickly sliced bananas and 6 rashers smoked streaky bacon in 1 tablespoon sunflower oil until golden. Cut the bacon into thin strips and arrange on a serving plate with the chicken, corn cobs and bananas.

caribbean chicken skewers & salsa

Serves **4**

Preparation time **30 minutes**,
  plus marinating

Cooking time **35–42 minutes**

4 tablespoons **pineapple
  juice** (from can below)

1 tablespoon **tomato ketchup**

1 teaspoon **paprika**

½ teaspoon **ground cinnamon**

large pinch **ground allspice**

4 boneless, skinless **chicken
  breasts**, cubed

1 **red pepper**, cored,
  deseeded, cut into chunks

1 **orange pepper**, cored,
  deseeded, cut into chunks

For the salsa

220 g (7½ oz) can **pineapple
  rings in natural juice**,
  drained

2 **tomatoes**, diced

100 g (3½ oz) **frozen
  sweetcorn**, just thawed

½ **red chilli**, deseeded, finely
  chopped (optional)

1.5 cm (¾ inch) piece **root
  ginger**, finely chopped

small bunch **fresh coriander**,
  roughly chopped

Put the pineapple juice into a bowl. Stir the ketchup and spices into the juice, add the chicken and toss together. Leave to marinate for at least 30 minutes.

Meanwhile, to make the salsa, finely chop the pineapple rings and put in a bowl with the tomatoes and sweetcorn. Add the chilli (if using), ginger and half the coriander and toss together.

Thread the pepper chunks on to 12 wooden or metal skewers, alternating with the chicken pieces. Sprinkle the skewers with the remaining chopped coriander. Grill the skewers under a preheated hot grill for 10–12 minutes, turning several times until well browned and the chicken is cooked through.

Serve the skewers with brown rice and spoonfuls of the salsa.

For Caribbean rice salad, as an accompaniment to the skewers, put 200 g (7 oz) easy-cook brown rice in a saucepan of boiling water and cook for 25–30 minutes or until tender. Drain the rice, rinse well with cold water then drain again. Mix it with the salsa, 150–175 g (5–7 oz) diced cooked chicken, 4 tablespoons toasted desiccated coconut and 1 deseeded and diced red pepper.

peppered chicken & aubergines

Serves **4**
Preparation time **15 minutes**
Cooking time **15 minutes**

2 tablespoons **sunflower oil**
6 boneless, skinless **chicken
    thighs,** cut into cubes
1 large **aubergine**, diced
1 **red onion**, sliced
2 **garlic cloves**, finely chopped
2 tablespoons **medium hot
    curry paste**
½ teaspoon **black
    peppercorns**, roughly
    crushed
small bunch **fresh coriander**,
    to garnish

Heat the oil in a large frying pan, add the chicken and
aubergine and fry, stirring for 5 minutes until the
aubergine is just beginning to soften. Stir in the onion
and garlic and fry for 5 more minutes, stirring until the
onion and chicken is just beginning to brown.

Mix in the curry paste and peppercorns and fry for
5 minutes until the chicken is a rich golden brown
and cooked through when tested (see page 11). Tear
the coriander into pieces and sprinkle over the top.
Serve immediately with bowls of tomato salad, yogurt
and rice.

For curried chicken with mixed vegetables, use a
small aubergine rather than a large one, then mix in
1 diced courgette and 1 diced and deseeded green
pepper along with the onion. Finish with 100 g (3½ oz)
spinach and cook for 2 minutes until just wilted.

penne with chicken livers

Serves **4**
Preparation time **10 minutes**
Cooking time **10–15 minutes**

1 **yellow pepper**, cored,
   deseeded
300 g (10 oz) **penne**
1 tablespoon **olive oil**
25 g (1 oz) **butter**
1 **red onion**, sliced
250 g (8 oz) **chicken livers**,
   trimmed
1 **rosemary sprig**, chopped
salt and **pepper**
25 g (1 oz) **Parmesan
   cheese**, grated, to serve

Roast the yellow pepper in a hot oven or under a preheated hot grill, skin-side up, until the skin is blistered and black. Place in a plastic bag and allow to cool, then peel off the skin. Cut the flesh into strips.

Cook the penne in lightly salted boiling water, according to the packet instructions.

Meanwhile, heat the oil and butter in a large frying pan, add the sliced onion and chicken livers and cook over a high heat until browned all over. Add the rosemary, the strips of yellow pepper and seasoning. Do not overcook the livers as they will become dry and hard – they are best when still pink in the middle.

Mix the chicken liver mixture with the cooked pasta and toss well. Serve immediately with the Parmesan.

For chicken-liver crostini, make up the liver mixture as above but cut the pepper and onion into dice rather than slices. Instead of tossing the liver mixture with pasta, spoon it onto toasted slices of ciabatta bread that have been rubbed with a cut clove of garlic and drizzled with a little oil. Sprinkle with parmesan shavings and serve warm or cold.

food for
friends

spiced chicken with yogurt crust

Serves **4**

Preparation time **30 minutes**, plus marinating

Cooking time **1 hour 20 minutes**

1.5 kg (3 lb) **whole chicken**

2.5 cm (1 inch) piece **root ginger**, sliced

2 small **green chillies**

small bunch **fresh coriander**, plus extra to garnish

4 **garlic cloves**, peeled

200 g (7 oz) **low-fat natural yogurt**

grated rind and juice of 1 **lemon**

1 teaspoon each **ground garam masala** and **ground turmeric**

1 teaspoon **cumin seeds**, roughly crushed

1 teaspoon **salt**

50 g (2 oz) **butter**, melted

Slash each chicken leg and breast 2–3 times with a sharp knife, then put the chicken in a large plastic bag. Finely chop the ginger, chillies, coriander and garlic in a food processor or with a large knife. Mix into the yogurt, then stir in the lemon rind and juice, spices and salt. Spoon the mixture into the plastic bag, seal well and refrigerate for 4 hours (or overnight).

Allow the chicken to come to room temperature for 1 hour, then remove it from the bag (with a thick coating) and put it in a roasting tin. Spoon 4 tablespoons of water into the base of the tin. Drizzle the chicken with butter.

Roast, uncovered, in a preheated oven, 190°C (375°F), Gas Mark 5, for 1 hour 20 minutes, spooning a little more of the yogurt marinade over the chicken once or twice.

Test the chicken (see page 11). When cooked through, transfer it to a serving dish, garnish with coriander and serve with pilau rice.

For nectarine chutney, as an accompaniment, fry 1 finely chopped red onion in 1 tablespoon of sunflower oil for 5 minutes. Add 6 roughly crushed cardamom pods, then mix in 400 g (13 oz) nectarines and 2 tablespoons each of red wine vinegar, light muscovado sugar and water. Cover and simmer for 10 minutes.

classic coq au vin

Serves **4**

Preparation time **25 minutes**

Cooking time **1 hour 20 minutes**

25 g (1 oz) **plain flour**

8 mixed **chicken thigh** and **drumstick joints**

2 tablespoons **olive oil**

375 g (12 oz) **shallots,** halved if large

125 g (4 oz) **smoked streaky bacon**

2 **garlic cloves**, finely chopped

4 tablespoons **brandy** or **cognac**

300 ml (½ pint) **cheap burgundy red wine**

200 ml (7 fl oz) **chicken stock** (see page 10)

2 teaspoons **tomato purée**

fresh or dried **bouquet garni**

salt and **pepper**

For the garlic croûtons

25 g (1 oz) **butter**

1 tablespoon **olive oil**

1 **garlic clove**, finely chopped

½ stick **French bread**, thinly sliced

Mix the flour on a plate with a little seasoning, then use to coat the chicken joints. Heat the oil in a large shallow flameproof casserole (or frying pan and transfer chicken to a casserole dish later), add the chicken and cook over a high heat until golden on all sides. Lift out on to a plate.

Fry the shallots and bacon until golden, then stir in the garlic and return the chicken to the casserole. Pour over the brandy or cognac and when bubbling flame with a long taper. As soon as the flames subside, pour in the red wine and stock, then mix in the tomato purée and bouquet garni. Season, then cover the casserole and transfer to a preheated oven, 180°C (350°F), Gas Mark 4, and cook for 1¼ hours until tender.

When the chicken is cooked, pour the liquid from the casserole into a saucepan and boil for 5 minutes to reduce and thicken slightly, if liked. Return the liquid to the casserole.

Heat the butter and oil in a frying pan for the croûtons, add the garlic and cook for 1 minute, then add the bread slices in a single layer. Fry on both sides until golden. Serve the coq au vin in shallow bowls topped with the croûtons.

For flamed chicken with calvados & apple, fry the chicken as above, adding 4 tablespoons calvados instead of the brandy. Pour in 300 ml (½ pint) cider in place of the red wine and omit the tomato purée. Transfer to a casserole dish and add 1 cored and thickly sliced Granny Smith dessert apple. Continue as above.

chicken with preserved lemons

Serves **4–5**
Preparation time **20 minutes**
Cooking time **1 hour
45 minutes**

2 tablespoons **olive oil**
1 **onion**, finely chopped
3 **garlic cloves**
1 teaspoon **ground ginger**
1½ teaspoons **ground
cinnamon**
large pinch **saffron threads**,
toasted, crushed
1.75 kg (3½ lb) **whole
chicken**
750 ml (1¼ pints) **chicken
stock** (see page 10) or
water
150 g (5 oz) large **black
olives**, rinsed, soaked
(optional)
1 **preserved lemon**, chopped
large bunch **coriander**, finely
chopped
large bunch **parsley**, finely
chopped
salt and **pepper**

Heat the oil in a frying pan, add the onion and fry
gently, stirring frequently until softened and golden.

Meanwhile, using a pestle and mortar, crush the garlic
with a pinch of salt, then work in the ginger, cinnamon,
saffron and a little pepper. Stir into the onions, cook
until fragrant, then remove from the pan and spread
over the chicken.

Put the chicken into a heavy saucepan or flameproof
casserole that it just fits, heat gently and brown the
chicken for about 2–3 minutes, turning often. Add the
stock or water, and bring to just simmering point. Cover
and simmer gently for about 1¼ hours, turning the
chicken over 2–3 times.

Add the olives, preserved lemon, coriander and parsley
to the pan. Cover and cook for about 15 minutes until
the chicken is very tender. Taste the sauce – if the
flavour needs to be more concentrated, transfer the
chicken to a warmed serving dish, cover and keep
warm, and boil the cooking juices to a rich sauce. Tilt
the pan and skim off any surplus fat, then pour over
the chicken. Serve with couscous, if liked.

For chicken & tomato tagine, reduce the stock or
water to 450 ml (¾ pint) and add a 400 ml (13 oz)
can of chopped tomatoes. Cover and simmer as
above. Omit the olives and lemon instead adding
75 g (3 oz) thickly sliced okra and the coriander and
parsley as above for the last 5 minutes of cooking.
Serve with rice or warmed Arab flat breads.

chicken with 30 garlic cloves

Serves **4**

Preparation time **25 minutes**

Cooking time **1 hour
30 minutes**

4 **chicken leg** and **thigh
joints**

25 g (1 oz) **butter**

1 tablespoon **olive oil**

250 g (8 oz) **shallots**, halved
if large

2 tablespoons **plain flour**

200 ml (7 fl oz) **dry white
wine**

200 ml (7 fl oz) **chicken stock**
(see page 10)

2 teaspoons **Dijon mustard**

3 **garlic bulbs**

small bunch **thyme**

4 tablespoons **crème frâiche**,
optional

salt and **pepper**

Fry the chicken in the butter and oil in a frying pan, until golden on both sides. Transfer to a large casserole dish.

Fry the shallots until softened and lightly browned. Stir in the flour, then gradually mix in the wine, stock, mustard and seasoning. Bring to the boil, stirring.

Separate the garlic cloves but do not peel them. Count out 30 cloves and add to the casserole dish with 3–4 thyme stems. Pour over the wine mix, then cover and cook in a preheated oven, 180°C (350°F), Gas Mark 4, for 1½ hours.

Stir in the crème fraîche, if liked and serve with mashed potatoes and green beans.

For baked chicken with flageolet beans & parsley,

fry the chicken and onion as above with just 2 finely chopped garlic cloves added to the onion. Mix with the wine, stock, mustard and seasoning, then add a 400 g (13 oz) can drained flageolet beans to the casserole with the thyme. Remove the thyme at the end and stir in 4 tablespoons chopped parsley, omitting the crème fraîche.

chicken mole

Serves **4**
Preparation time **25 minutes**
Cooking time **45 minutes**

1 tablespoon **sunflower oil**
500 g (1 lb) **minced chicken**
1 **onion**, roughly chopped
2 **garlic cloves**, finely
  chopped
1 teaspoon **smoked paprika**
½ teaspoon **dried chilli seeds**
1 teaspoon **cumin seeds**,
  roughly crushed
400 g (13 oz) can **chopped
  tomatoes**
400 g (13 oz) can **red kidney
  beans**
150 ml (¼ pint) **chicken stock**
  (see page 10)
1 tablespoon **dark brown
  sugar**
50 g (2 oz) **dark chocolate**,
  diced
salt and **pepper**

Heat the oil in a saucepan, add the chicken and onion and fry, breaking up the mince with a wooden spoon until browned. Mix in the garlic, paprika, chilli and cumin seeds and cook for 1 minute.

Stir in the tomatoes, beans, stock and sugar, then mix in the chocolate and seasoning. Cover and simmer gently for 45 minutes, stirring occasionally. Spoon the chilli into bowls to serve

For mole toppings, to add to the dish, mix together ½ finely chopped red onion, ½ cored, deseeded, diced red pepper, 1 halved, stoned, peeled and diced avocado, the rind and juice of 1 lime and a small bunch of roughly chopped coriander. Spoon into a serving bowl. Put 100 g (3½ oz) of tortilla chips in a second bowl and 100 g (3½ oz) grated mature Cheddar cheese in a third. Allow guests to add their own combination of toppings to the mole.

chicken stacks

Serves **4**
Preparation time **10 minutes**
Cooking time **50–55 minutes**

4 x 125 g (4 oz) boneless,
  skinless **chicken breasts**
1 small bunch **sage**
4 slices **prosciutto ham**
4 slices **fontina cheese**, rind
  removed
olive oil, for drizzling
salt and **pepper**

Heat a griddle pan (or ordinary frying pan). Lay the chicken breasts flat on a board and, using a sharp knife, slice each one horizontally to give 3 flat pieces.

Cook 4 pieces of chicken for 5 minutes on each side. When cooked, arrange these on an oiled baking sheet – these will form the base of the stacks. Put a few sage leaves on top of each one and season.

Cut each length of prosciutto in half and cook 4 pieces for 4 minutes on each side. Place these on top of the chicken. Cut each slice of fontina in half. Top each chicken and prosciutto stack with a piece of cheese.

Griddle or fry the remaining chicken and prosciutto and stack up as before with the cheese and sage, completing each stack with a final layer of chicken. Place the baking sheet in a preheated oven, 180°C (350°F), Gas Mark 4, and cook until the cheese is soft, about 5–8 minutes.

Drizzle with a little olive oil, sprinkle with salt and pepper and garnish with a few sage leaves. Serve with freshly cooked pasta tossed in butter and black pepper.

For tricolore stacks, prepare and fry the chicken as above layering up with 1 extra large sliced tomato and 1 small sliced aubergine, that have both been fried in 1–2 tablespoons olive oil. Instead of adding sage leaves, drizzle each layer with a little pesto. Garnish with basil leaves and parmesan shavings and serve with a green salad.

sherried chicken strogonoff

Serves **4**

Preparation time **10 minutes**

Cooking time **8–10 minutes**

25 g (1 oz) **butter**

2 tablespoons **sunflower oil**

4 boneless, skinless **chicken breasts**, cut into long, thin slices

2 **onions**, thinly sliced

1 teaspoon **paprika**

2 teaspoons **mild mustard**

6 tablespoons **dry** or **medium dry sherry**

6 tablespoons **water**

6 tablespoons **soured cream**

salt and **pepper**

Heat the butter and oil in a large frying pan, then add the chicken and onions and fry over a medium heat for 6–7 minutes, stirring until the chicken and onions are a deep golden colour.

Stir in the paprika, then add the mustard, sherry, water and seasoning. Cook for 2–3 minutes until the chicken is cooked through, then add the cream and swirl together. Spoon on to plates and serve with rice and green beans.

For chicken & fennel strogonoff, fry the sliced chicken breasts in the butter and oil as above, replacing one of the onions with 1 small, thinly sliced fennel bulb. When golden, add the mustard (but no paprika), 6 tablespoons Pernod instead of the sherry, flaming with a taper, then the water as above. Cook for 2–3 minutes, then add 6 tablespoons crème fraîche, stir until just melted, then serve.

chicken kievs

Serves **4**

Preparation time **40 minutes**, plus freezing and chilling

Cooking time **20 minutes**

125 g (4 oz) **butter**, at room temperature

2 tablespoons chopped **chives**

1 tablespoon chopped **parsley**

2 teaspoons chopped **tarragon** (optional)

1 **garlic clove**, finely chopped

2 teaspoons **lemon juice**

4 boneless, skinless **chicken breasts**, each about 100 g (5 oz)

2 tablespoons **plain flour**

125 g (4 oz) **fresh breadcrumbs**

2 **eggs**

3 tablespoons **sunflower oil**

pepper

Beat the butter with the herbs, garlic, lemon juice and a little pepper. Spoon into a line about 25 cm (10 inches) long on a sheet of clingfilm or foil, then roll up into a neat log shape. Freeze for 15 minutes.

Meanwhile, put one of the chicken breasts between two large sheets of clingfilm and beat with a rolling pin until it forms a rectangle about 3 mm (⅛ inch) thick, being careful not to make any holes in the chicken. Repeat with the other chicken breasts.

Cut the herb butter into 4 pieces and put one on each chicken breast. Fold in the sides, then the top and bottom, to make a tight parcel.

Put the flour on a plate and the breadcrumbs on a second plate, and beat the eggs in a shallow dish. Roll the kievs in the flour, then coat in the egg and roll in the breadcrumbs. Put back on to the empty flour plate and chill for 1 hour (longer if you have time).

Heat the oil in a large frying pan, add the kievs and cook over a medium heat for 5 minutes, turning until evenly browned. Transfer to a baking sheet, then complete cooking in a preheated oven, 200°C (400°F), Gas Mark 6, for 15 minutes or until the chicken is cooked through. Serve with new potatoes and braised red cabbage.

For chicken, garlic & sun-dried tomato kievs, chop 50 g (2 oz) drained sun-dried tomatoes in oil and stir into 150 g (5 oz) garlic and herb cream cheese. Divide between the flattened chicken breasts, then shape, chill and cook as above.

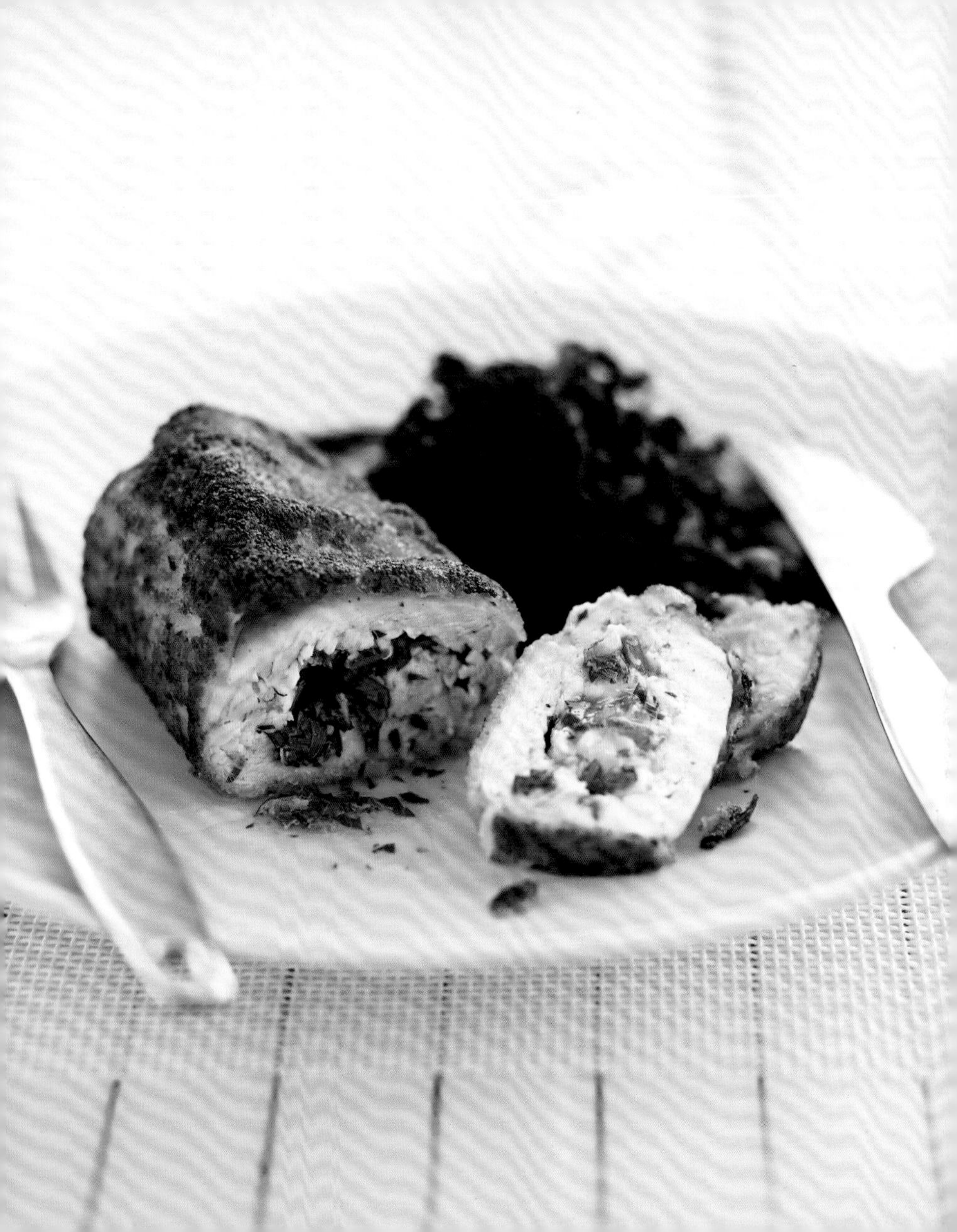

moroccan chicken & harissa

Serves **4**
Preparation time **20 minutes**
Cooking time **35 minutes**

1 **onion**, very finely chopped
2 teaspoons **paprika**
1 teaspoon **cumin seeds**
4 x 125 g (4 oz) boneless,
   skinless **chicken breasts**
1 bunch **fresh coriander**,
   finely chopped
4 tablespoons **lemon juice**
3 tablespoons **olive oil**
salt and **pepper**

For the harissa
4 **red peppers**
4 large **red chillies**
2 **garlic cloves**, crushed
½ teaspoon **coriander seeds**
1 teaspoon **caraway seeds**
5 tablespoons **olive oil**

Make the harissa by heating a griddle pan (or ordinary frying pan). Add the whole red peppers and cook for 15 minutes, turning occasionally. The skins will blacken and start to lift. Place the peppers in a plastic bag, seal the bag and set aside for a while (this encourages them to 'sweat', making it easier to remove their skins). When cool enough to handle, remove the skin, cores and seeds from the peppers and place the flesh in a blender or food processor.

Remove the skin, cores and seeds from the red chillies in the same way and add the chilli flesh to the blender, together with the garlic, coriander and caraway seeds and olive oil. Process in the blender to a smooth paste. If not required immediately, place the harissa in a sealable container and pour a thin layer of olive oil over the top. Cover with a lid and refrigerate.

Clean the griddle pan (or ordinary frying pan) and reheat it. Place the onion in a bowl, add the paprika and cumin seeds and mix together. Rub the onion and spice mixture into the chicken breasts. Cook the chicken for 10 minutes on each side, turning once. When cooked, remove from the pan.

Place the coriander in a bowl and add the lemon juice, olive oil and a little seasoning. Add the chicken to the bowl and toss well. Serve with rice and the harissa.

For a spinach salad, as an accompaniment, rinse and tear 400 g (13 oz) spinach and add to a pan with any residual water. Cover and cook for 1–2 minutes until wilted. Stir in 1 clove chopped garlic, 100 g (3½ oz) Greek yogurt, salt and pepper. Warm and serve.

chicken & mushroom lasagne

Serves **4–6**
Preparation time **45 minutes**
Cooking time **1 hour
25 minutes**

8 **chicken thighs**
150 ml (¼ pint) **dry white wine**
300 ml (½ pint) **chicken stock**
(see page 10)
few stems **thyme**
2 tablespoons **olive oil**
2 **onions**, thinly sliced
2 **garlic cloves**, finely chopped
100 g (3½ oz) **exotic
mushrooms**
125 g (4 oz) **shiitake
mushrooms**, sliced
50 g (2 oz) **butter**
50 g (2 oz) **plain flour**
200 ml (7 fl oz) **double cream**
250 g (8 oz) pack of
6 **fresh lasagne sheets**
40 g (1½ oz) **Parmesan
cheese**, freshly grated
salt and **pepper**

Pack the chicken thighs into the base of a saucepan, add the wine, stock, thyme and a little seasoning. Bring to the boil, then cover and simmer for 45 minutes until tender.

Meanwhile, heat the oil in a frying pan, add the onions and fry for 5 minutes until just turning golden. Mix in the garlic and cook for 2–3 minutes, then stir in the mushrooms and fry for 2–3 minutes until golden.

Lift the chicken out of the pan, drain and set aside. Pour the stock into a measuring jug. Make up to 600 ml (1 pint) with water if needed. Wash and dry the pan, then melt the butter in it. Stir in the flour, then gradually whisk in the stock and bring to the boil, stirring until thickened and smooth. Stir in the cream and adjust the seasoning, if needed.

Soak the lasagne sheets in boiling water for 5 minutes. Cut the skin and bones away from the chicken and dice the meat. Drain the lasagne sheets.

Pour a thin layer of sauce into the base of a 20 x 28 x 5 cm (8 x 11 x 2 inch) ovenproof dish or roasting tin, then cover with 2 sheets of the lasagne. Spoon over half the mushroom mixture and half the chicken, then cover with a thin layer of sauce. Repeat the layers, then cover with the remaining lasagne and sauce. Sprinkle with the Parmesan and set aside until required.

Cook in a preheated oven, 190°C (375°F), Gas Mark 5, for 40 minutes until piping hot and the top is golden. Serve with salad and garlic bread.

griddled tandoori chicken

Serves **4**

Preparation time **10 minutes**,
  plus marinating

Cooking time **16–20 minutes**

4 x 125 g (4 oz) boneless,
  skinless **chicken breasts**

4 tablespoons **tandoori paste**
  or **powder**

2 **red onions**, finely sliced

4 **tomatoes**, finely sliced

1 bunch **fresh coriander**,
  roughly chopped

4 tablespoons **lemon juice**

4 tablespoons **olive oil**

lemon wedges, griddled
  (optional), to serve

salt and **pepper**

Using a sharp knife, make a series of small slashes in the flesh of the chicken breasts and rub in the tandoori paste or powder. Leave to marinate in the refrigerator overnight.

Heat a griddle pan (or ordinary frying pan). Cook the marinated chicken breasts for 8–10 minutes on each side, allowing the authentic tandoori charred colour to appear, or until cooked throroughly.

Mix the red onions, tomatoes and coriander together with the lemon juice, olive oil and seasoning in a small bowl. Serve the salad with the tandoori chicken, accompanied by lemon wedges, griddled if liked.

For griddled harissa chicken, rub the slashed chicken with 4 teaspoons harissa paste instead of the tandoori paste or powder. Marinate then fry. Soak 200 g (7 oz) cous cous in 450 ml (¾ pint) boiling water for 5 minutes. Stir in 2 tablespoons olive oil, 3 tablespoons fresh chopped coriander and seasoning. Serve with lemon wedges.

cidered chicken puff pie

Serves **4**
Preparation time **40 minutes**
Cooking time **1 hour
20 minutes**

8 **chicken thighs**
300 ml (½ pint) **dry cider**
300 ml (½ pint) **chicken stock**
(see page 10)
2 small **leeks**, slit, rinsed,
sliced
50 g (2 oz) **butter**
50 g (2 oz) **plain flour**
1 tablespoon chopped
tarragon
2 tablespoons chopped
parsley
500 g (1 lb) **puff pastry**
flour, for dusting
1 **egg**, beaten, to glaze
salt and **pepper**

Pack the chicken thighs into a saucepan, pour over the cider and stock, then season. Cover and simmer for 45 minutes.

Lift the chicken on to a plate, and simmer the leeks in the stock for 4–5 minutes. Strain the leeks, reserving the stock in a measuring jug. Make up the stock to 600 ml (1 pint) with water, if needed.

Wash and dry the pan, then melt the butter in it. Stir in the flour, then gradually whisk in the stock and bring to the boil, stirring until thickened. Mix in the herbs and season.

Dice the chicken, discarding the skin and bones. Put into a 1.2 litre (2 pint) pie dish with the leeks. Pour over the sauce.

Roll out the pastry on a floured surface until a little larger than the top of the pie dish. Cut 4 strips about 1 cm (½ inch) wide and stick along the rim with a little egg. Brush the top of the strip with egg, then press the pastry lid in place. Trim off the excess and crimp the edge. Cut leaves from the excess and add.

Glaze the pastry lid and bake in a preheated oven, 200°C (400°F), Gas Mark 6, for 30 minutes until golden.

For chicken, frankfurter & corn puff pie, cook 6 chicken thighs as above, and add the meat to the pie dish with 4 thickly sliced, chilled frankfurters. Replace the leeks with a 200 g (7 oz) drained can of sweetcorn. Omit the herbs from the sauce and flavour with 1 teaspoon English mustard, then continue as above.

thai red chicken curry

Serves **4**

Preparation time **15 minutes**

Cooking time **35 minutes**

3 **shallots**, finely chopped

3 **garlic cloves**, finely chopped

1 tablespoon **sunflower oil**

2 tablespoons **red Thai curry paste**

2 teaspoons **galangal paste** (from a jar)

400 ml (14 fl oz) can **low-fat coconut milk**

2 teaspoons **fish sauce**

1 teaspoon **light muscovado sugar**

3 dried **kaffir lime leaves**

6 **chicken thighs**, skinned, boned, diced

Thai basil leaves, optional

Fry the shallots and garlic in the oil in a medium saucepan for 3–4 minutes until softened. Stir in the curry paste and galangal and cook for 1 minute. Mix in the coconut milk, fish sauce, sugar and lime leaves and bring to the boil.

Stir in the chicken, then cover and simmer for 30 minutes, stirring occasionally until the chicken is cooked through. Stir in the basil leaves, if liked, and serve in bowls with boiled rice.

For Thai green chicken curry, make the curry as above, adding 2 peeled and finely chopped lemon grass stems when frying the shallots and garlic. Stir in 2 tablespoons green Thai curry paste, then the remaining ingredients as above. Finish by stirring in the grated rind of 1 lime and lime juice to taste. Garnish with fresh coriander.

baked chicken in a salt crust

Serves **4**
Preparation time **20 minutes**
Cooking time **2 hours**

3 kg (6 lb) **salt**
1.5 kg (3 lb) **whole chicken**
1 **garlic bulb**
3–4 stems **rosemary**
150 ml (¼ pint) **water**

For the red pepper ketchup
4 whole **red peppers** from a
   jar of roasted peppers in
   water, drained
1 tablespoon **sweet Thai chilli
   dipping sauce**
1 tablespoon **olive oil**
1 tablespoon **balsamic
   vinegar**
black pepper, to taste

Line an ovenproof casserole dish or roasting tin (large enough to hold the salt and chicken) with two large pieces of foil. Pour a thin layer of salt into the base, then sit the chicken on top. Cut the garlic in half through the centre, then put both halves into the body cavity of the chicken with one of the rosemary stems. Tear the leaves from the other stems and sprinkle over the chicken.

Pour the remaining salt over the chicken, pulling up the foil to contain the salt in an even thickness around the chicken. Drizzle the measured water over the top, then spread the dampened salt into an even layer over the breast. Seal the edges of the foil tightly.

Bake in a preheated oven, 190°C (375°F), Gas Mark 5, for 2 hours. Loosen the edge of the foil, then lift the package out. Open the foil and crack the salt crust away from the chicken.

To make the ketchup, remove one of the cooked half garlic bulbs from inside the chicken cavity, discarding the papery skins, and put into a food processor with the other ketchup ingredients. Purée until smooth. Brush the salt off the chicken with a pastry brush, then carve normally and serve with the ketchup, salad and warm ciabatta bread.

For baked chicken with aïoli, cook the chicken as above, then take all the garlic cloves out of their skins and pound to a paste in a pestle and mortar with a pinch of the baking salt. Mix with 150 g (5 oz) good-quality bought mayonnaise and season with coarsely crushed black pepper.

chicken with chilli and ginger jam

Serves **4**
Preparation time **5 minutes**
Cooking time **25 minutes**

4 x 125 g (4 oz) boneless
   chicken breasts
rice noodles, to serve
fresh coriander leaves, to
   garnish

For the chilli and ginger jam
125 g (4 oz) **chillies**, cored,
   deseeded, chopped
1 **garlic clove**, crushed
1 **onion**, chopped
5 cm (2 inch) piece **root
   ginger**, peeled, chopped
125 ml (4 fl oz) **white vinegar**
500 g (1 lb) **sugar**

To make the chilli and ginger jam, place the chopped chillies, garlic, chopped onion and ginger in a small saucepan. Add the white vinegar and sugar. Bring to the boil, then reduce the heat and allow to simmer for 15 minutes. The mixture should be thick, sticky and jam-like, and will become more so as it cools.

Meanwhile, heat a griddle pan (or ordinary frying pan). Cook the chicken breasts, skin side down, for 8–10 minutes. Turn the chicken over and cook for a further 8–10 minutes, or until cooked thoroughly.

Serve the chicken on a bed of noodles, with the chilli and ginger jam poured over the top, and garnish with coriander leaves. Store any remaining chilli jam in the refrigerator, covered, for up to 1 week.

For chicken salad with chilli dressing, cook the chicken as above. Mix ½ diced cucumber in a salad bowl with ½ thinly sliced red onion, 200 g (7 oz) halved cherry tomatoes, 2 Little Gem lettuces, torn into leaves and a small bunch of mint, torn into pieces. Fork the juice of 2 limes, 1 tablespoon Thai chilli dipping sauce, 1 tablespoon soy sauce, 1 teaspoon dark brown sugar together. Add the chicken to the salad and drizzle with dressing.

chicken and barley risotto

Serves **4**

Preparation time **15 minutes**

Cooking time **1 hour
10 minutes**

2 tablespoons **olive oil**

6 boneless, skinless **chicken
thighs**, diced

1 **onion**, roughly chopped

2 **garlic cloves**, finely chopped

200 g (7 oz) **chestnut
mushrooms**, sliced

250 g (8 oz) **pearl barley**

200 ml (7 fl oz) **red wine**

1.2 litres (2 pints) **chicken
stock** (see page 10)

salt and **pepper**

To garnish

parsley, chopped

shavings of **Parmesan
cheese**

Heat the oil in a large frying pan, add the chicken and onion and fry for 5 minutes, stirring until lightly browned.

Stir in the garlic and mushrooms and fry for 2 minutes, then mix in the barley. Add the red wine, half the stock and plenty of seasoning, then bring to the boil, stirring. Cover and simmer for 1 hour, topping up with extra stock as needed until the barley is soft.

Spoon into shallow bowls and garnish with the parsley and Parmesan. Serve with garlic bread and salad.

For chicken & red rice risotto, fry the chicken and 1 chopped red onion as above. Add the garlic and 200 g (7 oz) skinned and diced tomatoes in place of the mushrooms. Stir in 250 g (8 oz) red Camargue rice, cook for 1 minute, then add the wine. Gradually add 1.2 litres (2 pints) of hot chicken stock, ladle by ladle as needed, only adding more once the rice has absorbed the previous ladleful. Cook for 25 minutes until the chicken and rice are tender. Top with 125 g (4 oz) crumbled St Agur or Roquefort cheese.

southern fried chicken

Serves **4**

Preparation time **25 minutes**

Cooking time **35–40 minutes**

500 g (1 lb) **sweet potatoes**, peeled

500 g (1 lb) **baking potatoes**, scrubbed

6 tablespoons **sunflower oil**

1½ teaspoons **smoked paprika**

1½ teaspoons **dried oregano**

1 teaspoon **dried mustard powder**

1 teaspoon **dried crushed red chillies**

4 tablespoons **plain flour**

2 **eggs**

2 tablespoons **water**

125 g (4 oz) **fresh breadcrumbs**

4 **chicken thigh** and **drumstick joints**

salt and **pepper**

Thickly slice the sweet and baking potatoes, then cut into thick wedges. Mix 3 tablespoons of the oil with 1 teaspoon paprika, 1 teaspoon oregano, ½ teaspoon mustard, ½ teaspoon chilli seeds and some salt in a large plastic bag or bowl. Add the potatoes and toss in the oil mixture.

Mix the remaining paprika, oregano, mustard, chilli seeds and seasoning with the flour on a large plate. Beat the eggs and measured water in a shallow dish and put the breadcrumbs on a second large plate.

Coat the chicken pieces in the flour mixture, then the beaten egg, then the breadcrumbs, until completely covered.

Heat a large roasting tin in the oven, 200°C (400°F), Gas Mark 6, for 5 minutes. Meanwhile, heat the remaining oil in a large frying pan, add the chicken and fry until pale golden. Transfer the chicken to the hot roasting tin, add the potatoes and roast for 30–35 minutes until the chicken is cooked through and the potatoes crisp and golden. Transfer to serving plates and serve with mayonnaise and salad.

For cheesy fried chicken escalopes, make up the vegetables as above, then mix the remaining paprika, chilli seeds and a little salt and pepper with the flour. Coat 4 skinless, boneless chicken breasts, each cut into thin flat slices, in the flour mixture, then in the beaten egg, then in 100 g (3½ oz) fresh breadcrumbs mixed with 2 tablespoons grated Parmesan cheese. Fry in the oil for 10–12 minutes until golden and cooked through.

chicken qdra

Serves **4**
Preparation time **15 minutes**
Cooking time **2 hours
  5 minutes**

2 tablespoons **olive oil**
8 boneless, skinless **chicken
  thighs**, cut into large chunks
2 **onions**, thinly sliced
2 **garlic cloves**, finely
  chopped
2 tablespoons **plain flour**
900 ml (1½ pints) **chicken
  stock** (see page 10)
grated rind and juice of
  1 **lemon**
2 large pinches **saffron
  threads**
1 **cinnamon stick**, halved
2 x 410 g (13½ oz) cans
  chickpeas, drained
500 g (1 lb) **potatoes**, cut
  into chunks
parsley or **mixed parsley and
  mint**, chopped, to garnish
salt and **pepper**

Heat the oil in a large frying pan, add the chicken and onions, frying in batches if needed for 5 minutes until golden.

Stir in the garlic, then mix in the flour. Add the stock, lemon rind and juice, saffron, cinnamon and plenty of seasoning and bring to the boil. Transfer to a tagine or casserole dish. Add the chickpeas and potatoes, mix together, then cover. Cook in a preheated oven, 180°C (350°F), Gas Mark 4, for 2 hours.

Stir, then sprinkle with the herbs. Spoon into shallow bowls and serve with warm pitta breads.

For saffron chicken with mixed vegetables, reduce the stock to 600 ml (1 pint) and add a 400 g (13 oz) can of chopped tomatoes. Add 1 can of chickpeas only, then mix in 125 g (4 oz) thickly sliced okra and 125 g (4 oz) thickly sliced green beans 10 minutes before the end of cooking.

chinese lemon chicken

Serves **4**

Preparation time **25 minutes**,
  plus marinating

Cooking time **12 minutes**

4 tablespoons **cornflour**

1 tablespoon **dry sherry**

1 **egg**

grated rind of **1 lemon**

2 large boneless, skinless
  chicken breasts, cut into
  thin crossway slices

6 tablespoons **sunflower oil**

For the lemon sauce

2 tablespoons **cornflour**

juice of **1 lemon**

2 tablespoons **dry sherry**

4 teaspoons **caster sugar**

300 ml (½ pint) **chicken stock**
  (see page 10)

3 **spring onions**, thinly sliced

salt and **pepper**

Mix the cornflour with the sherry and egg until smooth,
then stir in the lemon rind and a little seasoning. Add
the chicken slices and toss together, then leave to
marinate for 30 minutes.

Make the sauce by mixing the cornflour in a saucepan
with a little of the lemon juice until smooth. Stir in the
remaining lemon juice, sherry, sugar and seasoning.
Put the pan on the heat and gradually whisk in the
stock. Bring to the boil, whisking until clear, thickened
and smooth. Take off the heat and add the onions.

Add the oil to a wok or large frying pan, heat and, then
add the chicken a few pieces at a time and cook for
4–5 minutes, turning until golden and cooked through.
Lift the chicken out of the pan with a draining spoon,
put it on a plate lined with kitchen paper and keep it
hot. Cook the remaining chicken in the same way.

Reheat the sauce. Transfer the chicken to small bowls
lined with rice, spoon a little of the sauce over the top,
pour the remaining sauce into a separate bowl, then
hand round so that guests can add sauce to taste.

For salt & pepper chicken, omit the lemon rind from
the egg and cornflour batter, adding a large pinch
of salt and ½ teaspoon roughly crushed sichuan
peppercorns. Fry in oil as above and serve with
sweet Thai chilli dipping sauce.

italian chicken cushion

Serves **4**

Preparation time **30 minutes**

Cooking time **1 hour 30 minutes**

1.5 kg (3 lb) **whole chicken**, boned

400 g (13 oz) **Sicilian sausages** or **other gourmet flavoured sausages** (such as Parmesan and pancetta)

4 **spring onions**, finely chopped

1 large **whole red pepper**, from a jar of roasted peppers in water, drained, diced

75 g (3 oz) **sun-dried tomatoes** in oil, drained, roughly chopped

50 g (2 oz) pitted **olives**, roughly chopped

3 tablespoons chopped **basil**

50 g (2 oz) **fresh breadcrumbs**

1 **egg yolk**

1 tablespoon **olive oil** or **oil from the sun-dried tomato jar**

salt and **pepper**

Put the boned chicken on a large chopping board with the breast skin downwards, neaten up the edges with a knife and open out flat.

Slit the sausages lengthways, peel off the skins and put the meat into a large bowl. Add the onions, red pepper, sun-dried tomatoes, olives, basil, breadcrumbs, egg yolk and plenty of seasoning and mix with a wooden spoon. Spoon on to the centre of the chicken. Fold the legs, wings and remaining skin back into position so that the stuffing is enclosed. Tie with string like the spokes of a wheel, adjusting the string and patting into shape to form a round cushion.

Weigh the joint, then put it breast side up in a roasting tin. Drizzle with the oil and season lightly. Cover with foil and roast in a preheated oven, 190°C (375°F), Gas Mark 5, for 20 minutes per 500 g (1 lb) plus 20 minutes. Remove the foil for the last 30 minutes and baste the chicken once or twice with pan juices until a deep golden brown and cooked when tested (see page 11).

Allow to cool, remove the string and cut into wedge shapes. Serve with salad.

For chicken cushion with ginger & cranberries, use plain good-quality sausages rather than highly flavoured ones, remove the skins and mix with the chopped spring onions, red pepper, breadcrumbs and egg yolk as above, then flavour with a 3.5 cm (1½ inch) piece of grated root ginger, the grated rind of 1 small orange, 3 tablespoons chopped parsley and 50 g (2 oz) dried cranberries. Serve hot with roast potatoes.

chicken bisteeya

Serves **6**

Preparation time **40 minutes**

Cooking time **1 hour
50 minutes**

4 **chicken thigh** and
  drumstick joints

1 **onion**, chopped

1 **cinnamon stick**, halved

2.5 cm (1 inch) piece **root
  ginger**, finely chopped

¼ teaspoon **turmeric**

600 ml (1 pint) **water**

3 tablespoons chopped **fresh
  coriander**

3 tablespoons chopped
  parsley

40 g (1½ oz) **raisins**

40 g (1½ oz) **blanched
  almonds**, roughly chopped

4 **eggs**

200 g (7 oz) pack chilled **filo
  pastry**

65 g (2½ oz) **butter**, melted

salt and **pepper**

To garnish
icing sugar, sifted
ground cinnamon

Pack the chicken into a large saucepan and sprinkle the onion over the top, then add the cinnamon, ginger, turmeric and seasoning. Cover the chicken with the measured water. Cover and simmer for 1 hour until tender. Lift the chicken out of the stock and put on a plate to cool. Boil the stock rapidly for about 10 minutes until reduced to one-third.

Dice the chicken, discarding the skin and bones. Strain the stock into a jug. Discard the cinnamon stick, then add the herbs, raisins and almonds to the chicken. Whisk 200 ml (7 fl oz) stock with the eggs.

Brush a 23 cm (9 inch) springform tin with a little of the melted butter. Unroll the pastry, then place one of the sheets in the tin so that it half covers the base and drapes up over the side and hangs over the top of the tin. Add a second pastry sheet overlapping a little over the first and brush with a little melted butter. Continue adding pastry, brushing alternate sheets with melted butter until two-thirds of the pastry has been used and the tin is thickly covered.

Spoon in the chicken mixture, then cover with the eggs and stock. Arrange the remaining pastry over the top in a smooth layer, then fold in the sides in soft pleats, brushing layers of pastry with butter as you go. Brush the top layer with the remaining butter, then bake in a preheated oven, 180°C (350°F), Gas Mark 4, for 40–45 minutes until golden brown and the filling is set.

Leave to cool for 15 minutes, remove from the tin and transfer to a chopping board. Dust lightly with icing sugar and cinnamon and serve warm.

chicken risotto

Serves **6**
Preparation time **35 minutes**
Cooking time **2 hours**

1 kg (2 lb) **whole chicken**
2 litres (3½ pints) **water**
2 **celery sticks**
2 **onions**
2 **carrots**
3–4 tablespoons **olive oil**
7 tablespoons **white wine**
375 g (12 oz) **tomatoes**,
  skinned and mashed
500 g (1 lb) **risotto rice**
75 g (3 oz) **butter**, softened
75 g (3 oz) **Parmesan
  cheese**, freshly grated
1–2 tablespoons chopped
  parsley, to garnish
salt and **pepper**

Remove the bones from the chicken and place them in a large pan with the water. Add 1 celery stick, 1 onion, 1 carrot and seasoning. Cover and simmer for 1½ hours. Strain the stock and keep hot.

Meanwhile, dice the chicken meat, discarding all the skin. Finely chop the remaining celery, onion and carrot. Heat the oil, add the chopped vegetables and sauté until lightly coloured. Add the chicken and cook, stirring for 5 minutes. Add the wine and cook, stirring, until it has evaporated.

Add the tomatoes and season to taste. Cover and cook over a low heat for 20 minutes, adding a little of the hot chicken stock if the mixture becomes dry.

Add the rice, then add the hot stock, a large ladleful at a time, stirring until each addition is absorbed into the rice. Continue adding stock in this way, cooking for 20 minutes until the rice is creamy.

Remove from the heat, add the butter and Parmesan and fold in gently. Cover and leave the risotto to rest for a few minutes before serving, sprinkled with parsley.

For chicken risotto with wild mushrooms, make the stock as above then fry just the celery and onion in oil for the base of the risotto. Add the diced chicken and continue adding stock until the risotto is almost cooked. In a separate frying pan, melt half the butter then add 100 g (3½ oz) pack exotic mushrooms, 125 g (4 oz) sliced shiitake mushrooms and 2 cloves finely chopped garlic, stirring until golden. Stir the remaining butter and parmesan into the risotto, spoon into bowls and top with the mushrooms.

stilton-stuffed chicken with ham

Serves **4**
Preparation time **25 minutes**
Cooking time **30 minutes**

4 boneless, skinless **chicken
    breasts**, each about
    150 g (5 oz)
125 g (4 oz) **Stilton cheese**,
    rind removed
50 g (2 oz) **sun-dried
    tomatoes** in oil, drained
4 slices **Parma ham**
salt and **pepper**

Cut a slit through the side of each chicken breast,
then enlarge to make a small pocket. Cut the cheese
into 4 slices, then tuck one slice into each chicken
pocket with 1–2 pieces of tomato depending on
their size. Sprinkle the outside of the chicken breasts
with seasoning.

Wrap each chicken breast with a slice of Parma ham
and put in a roasting tin.

Bake in a preheated oven, 200°C (400°F), Gas Mark
6, for 30 minutes until the chicken is cooked when
tested (see page 11). Thickly slice the chicken or
leave whole if preferred. Transfer to serving plates
and serve with purple sprouting broccoli and buttery
new potatoes.

For chicken cordon bleu, slit the chicken as above,
then fill with 125 g (4 oz) Gruyère cheese with its rind
removed and cut into 4 slices, and 2 halved slices of
smoked ham. Secure the pockets closed with cocktail
sticks, then fry in 25 g (1 oz) butter and 1 tablespoon
olive oil for 15 minutes, turning the chicken until
golden and cooked through. Deglaze the pan with
150 ml (¼ pint) white wine or stock and cook for
3–4 minutes until the chicken is cooked through. Stir
in 4 tablespoons double cream, then remove the
cocktail sticks and serve.

chicken with pimento pureé

Serves **8**
Preparation time **15 minutes**,
   plus cooling
Cooking time **1 hour**
   45 minutes–2 hours
   15 minutes

2 kg (4 lb) **whole chicken**
1 **onion**, quartered
1 **carrot**, sliced
2 **celery sticks**, sliced
4 **juniper berries**, crushed
1 **bay leaf**
4–6 stalks **parsley**
6 **peppercorns**, lightly
   crushed
courgette slices, griddled, to
   serve (optional)
parsley, chopped, to garnish
salt

For the pimento pureé
250 g (8 oz) canned
   pimentos, drained, rinsed,
   chopped
1 tablespoon **tomato purée**
2 tablespoons **mango
   chutney**
200 ml (7 fl oz) **low-fat
   natural yogurt**
salt and **pepper**

Put the chicken, onion, carrot, celery, juniper berries, bay leaf, parsley, peppercorns and salt into a saucepan. Cover with water. Bring to the boil, cover the saucepan and simmer for 1½–2 hours, or until the chicken is cooked when tested (see page 11). Leave the chicken to cool in the stock. Lift out the chicken, drain and dry it. Reserve the stock, discarding the bay leaf. Skin the chicken and slice the meat from the bones.

To make the pureé, put the pimentos, 2 tablespoons of the reserved chicken stock, tomato purée and chutney into a saucepan and bring to the boil. Transfer to a blender or food processor and blend until smooth. Set aside to cool. Blend the cooled pimento mixture with the yogurt and season to taste.

Arrange the chicken on a serving dish and pour over the sauce. Garnish with the parsley and serve with griddled courgettes, if liked.

For mini chicken meatballs with pimento pureé, mix 500 g (1 lb) minced chicken with 3 chopped spring onions, 2 cloves of finely chopped garlic, 1 egg yolk and seasoning. Shape into 20 small meatballs, chill for 30 minutes then fry in 1 tablespoon sunflower oil for 5 minutes. Transfer to a preheated oven 190°C (375°F) Gas Mark 5 for 15 minutes until cooked through. Serve with the sauce as above, rice and a tomato and onion salad.

lemon grass chicken & vegetables

Serves **4**

Preparation time **15 minutes**, plus soaking

Cooking time **about 10 minutes**

18 stalks **lemon grass**

8 boneless, skinless **chicken thighs**

1 **garlic clove**

2 **kaffir lime leaves**

2 tablespoons **soy sauce**

1 tablespoon **sesame oil**

1 **red pepper**, cored, deseeded, sliced

1 **green pepper**, cored, deseeded, sliced

375 g (12 oz) **sugar snap peas**

2 **pak choi**, quartered lengthways

Place 16 of the lemon grass stalks in a bowl of water and leave to soak for 1 hour. Chop the remaining 2 stalks.

Put the chicken, chopped lemon grass, garlic, lime leaves and half the soy sauce in a food processor and process until well combined. Divide the mixture into 16 portions and mould each portion around a piece of the soaked lemon grass.

Place on a baking sheet, drizzle with half the oil and cook under a hot grill for 4–5 minutes, turning occasionally, until golden and cooked through.

Heat the remaining oil in a wok or frying pan, add the vegetables and stir-fry for 2–3 minutes until just tender, then add the remaining soy sauce. Serve the stir-fried vegetables with the chicken.

For stir-fried lemon grass chicken, thinly slice 3 boneless skinless chicken breasts. Finely chop 2 lemon grass stalks, the garlic and lime leaves. Heat 2 teaspoons sesame oil and 2 teaspoons sunflower oil in a wok, add the chicken and stir-fry for 6–7 minutes. Add the chopped lemon grass, garlic and lime leaves then the vegetables and stir fry for 2–3 minutes until the vegetables are just tender and chicken is cooked through. Mix in 2 tablespoons soy sauce, 2 tablespoons dry sherry and 4 tablespoons water or stock, bring to the boil then serve with egg fried rice.

favourite
roasts

pot-roast chicken with vermouth

Serves **4**

Preparation time **20 minutes**

Cooking time **1 hour 40 minutes–1 hour 50 minutes**

1 tablespoon **olive oil**

200 g (7 oz) **shallots**, peeled, halved

2 slices **smoked back bacon**, diced

2 **garlic cloves**, finely chopped

500 g (1 lb) **baby new potatoes**

25 g (1 oz) **butter**

1.5 kg (3 lb) **whole chicken**

4 stems **celery**, each cut into 3 sections

250 g (8 oz) **baby carrots**, large ones halved

3 **bay leaves**

200 ml (7 fl oz) **dry vermouth**

200 ml (7 fl oz) **chicken stock** (see page 10)

2 tablespoons chopped **parsley**, to garnish (optional)

salt and **pepper**

Heat the oil in a large flameproof casserole, add the shallots and bacon and fry for 3–4 minutes over a medium heat until just beginning to brown. Add the garlic and potatoes and fry until just beginning to colour. Tip on to a plate.

Add the butter to the pan and, when melted, add the chicken, breast side downwards. Fry on each breast until golden, then turn over and fry the underside. Return the fried vegetables to the pan and tuck the celery and carrots around the sides of the chicken, adding the bay leaves and a little salt and pepper.

Pour in the vermouth and stock, then bring to the boil. Cover with a tight-fitting lid and transfer to a preheated oven, 190°C (375°F), Gas Mark 5, for 1¼ hours. Spoon the vermouth juices over the chicken, then cook uncovered for 20–30 minutes until golden and cooked when tested (see page 11).

Lift the chicken on to a serving plate, scoop the vegetables out with a draining spoon and nestle them around the chicken. Cover with foil and keep hot. Boil the remaining pan juices for about 5 minutes or until reduced by half, then pour into a jug and sprinkle the vegetables with the parsley, if liked. Carve as for a traditional roast and serve with the gravy.

For pot-roast chicken with cider & mustard, omit the garlic and vermouth, adding 200 ml (7 fl oz) dry cider and 2 teaspoons Dijon mustard. Continue as above.

198

roast chicken with lemon baste

Serves **4–5**

Preparation time **35 minutes**

Cooking time **1 hour 30 minutes**

1.75 kg (3½ lb) **whole chicken**

100 g (3½ oz) **full-fat cream cheese**

3 tablespoons **olive oil**

25 g (1 oz) **preserved lemon**, well drained, deseeded, finely chopped

25 g (1 oz) mixed fresh **basil** and **parsley**, finely chopped

3 **garlic cloves**, finely chopped

675 g (1 lb 6 oz) small **new potatoes**, scrubbed

250 g (8 oz) **chantenay carrots**, scrubbed

125 g (4 oz) **baby corn**

200 g (7 oz) **fine asparagus**, trimmed

200 ml (7 fl oz) **dry white wine**

200 ml (7 fl oz) **chicken stock** (see page 10)

salt and **cayenne pepper**

Remove the trussing elastic from the chicken and set aside. Insert a small sharp knife between the skin and the flesh at the top of one of the breasts, then enlarge to make a small slit. Slide a finger into the slit and gently move the finger to lift the skin away from the chicken breast and make a pocket, being careful not to tear the skin. Do the same from the base of the breast until the skin is completely loosened, then continue over the top of the leg. Repeat on the other chicken breast and leg.

Mix the cream cheese with 1 tablespoon of the oil, and add the lemon, herbs, garlic, salt and cayenne pepper. Lift small amounts of the cheese mix at a time on to a round-bladed knife and insert into the pocket beneath the chicken skin until it has all been added. Ease it into an even layer by pressing the outside of the skin.

Transfer the chicken to a roasting tin and reshape it by twisting the trussing elastic around the legs and parson's nose. Cover with oiled foil and roast in a preheated oven, 190°C (375°F), Gas Mark 5, for 50 minutes. Baste the chicken with the pan juices, then re-cover. Add the potatoes, carrots and remaining oil (but do not cover these with foil) and roast for 30 minutes, turning once. Remove the foil from the chicken, baste and add the corn and asparagus. Roast for 10 minutes until the asparagus is just tender and the chicken cooked when tested (see page 11).

Transfer to a serving plate, add the wine and stock to the roasting tin and bring to the boil on the hob, scraping up the residue in the tin and seasoning to taste. Strain into a jug and serve with the chicken.

roast chicken with spice rub

Serves **4**

Preparation time **20 minutes**

Cooking time **1 hour
20 minutes–1 hour
30 minutes**

1.5 kg (3 lb) **whole chicken**

3 tablespoons **olive oil**

1 teaspoon **fennel seeds**,
roughly crushed

1 teaspoon **cumin seeds**,
roughly crushed

1 teaspoon crushed **dried
red chillies**

1 teaspoon **dried oregano**

½ teaspoon **ground cinnamon**

625 g (1¼ lb) **baby new
potatoes**

2 **shallots**, finely chopped

2 **garlic cloves**, finely
chopped (optional)

150 g (5 oz) **fine green
beans**

juice of **1 lemon**

200 ml (7 fl oz) **chicken stock**
(see page 10)

small bunch **fresh coriander**
or **flat leaf parsley**, or mix of
the two, roughly chopped

salt and **pepper**

Put the chicken into a large roasting tin and drizzle with 2 tablespoons of the oil. Mix the crushed seeds, chillies, oregano and cinnamon with some salt and pepper, then sprinkle half over the chicken.

Cover the chicken loosely with foil, then roast in a preheated oven, 190°C (375°F), Gas Mark 5, for 40 minutes. Remove the foil and baste with the pan juices. Add the potatoes to the tin, toss in the juices, then cook uncovered for 40–50 minutes, basting and turning the potatoes once or twice until golden brown. Re-cover the chicken with foil if the spice rub begins to overbrown.

Meanwhile, heat the remaining oil in a small saucepan, add the shallots and garlic, if liked, and fry for 5 minutes until softened. Stir in the remaining spice rub and cook for 1 minute. Cook the green beans in a saucepan of boiling water for 5 minutes, then drain and toss in the shallot mixture with the lemon juice.

When the chicken is cooked (see page 11), add the green-bean mixture to the potatoes. Mix together, then add the stock and bring to the boil on the hob. Sprinkle with the herbs, carve the chicken and serve.

For roast chicken with herbes de Provence, roughly chop the leaves from 3 stems of rosemary, 3 stems of thyme and 2 lavender flowers. Mix with 1 teaspoon coarse salt and ¼ teaspoon roughly crushed coloured peppercorns. Sprinkle half over the chicken and the rest over the potatoes. Continue as above.

roast chicken with spiced roots

Serves **4**

Preparation time **30 minutes**

Cooking time **1 hour 20 minutes**

1.5 kg (3 lb) **whole chicken**

2 teaspoons **coriander seeds**

1 teaspoon **fennel seeds**

1 teaspoon **cumin seeds**

2 tablespoons **olive oil**

½ teaspoon **turmeric**

½ teaspoon **paprika**

2 **parsnips**

2 large **carrots**

2 **sweet potatoes**

1 large **onion**

8 **garlic cloves**, unpeeled

fresh coriander leaves, to garnish

For the gravy

2 tablespoons **plain flour**

450 ml (¾ pint) **chicken stock** (see page 10)

Place the chicken in a large roasting tin. Crush the seeds and put them in a large plastic bag with the oil, turmeric and paprika. Shake until well mixed. Spoon a little of the mixture over the chicken breast, then cover with foil.

Roast the chicken in a preheated oven, 190°C (375°F), Gas Mark 5, for 1 hour 20 minutes.

Cut the vegetables into large chunks, add to the bag of spiced oil and toss. Add to the roasting tin after 20 minutes of cooking the chicken, tucking some garlic cloves between the chicken legs and adding the rest to the vegetables. Cook for 1 hour until golden, turning the vegetables after 30 minutes and removing the foil from the chicken at this point.

Transfer the chicken and vegetables from the roasting tin to a large serving plate and keep warm. Garnish with coriander.

Drain the fat from the meat juices and stir in the flour. To make the gravy, put the roasting tin on the hob and cook for 1 minute, stirring. Gradually stir in the stock and bring to the boil. Strain into a jug and serve immediately with the carved chicken and vegetables.

For barbecued spiced chicken, mix the spices and oil in a plastic bag as above then add 8 boneless, skinless chicken thighs that have been slashed once or twice with a small knife. Toss together then cook over a medium hot barbecue for about 20 minutes, turning once or twice until browned and cooked through. Serve with cucumber raita and shredded lettuce.

roast chicken with sage & onion

Serves **4**

Preparation time **30 minutes**

Cooking time **1 hour
30 minutes–1 hour
40 minutes**

12 rashers **smoked streaky
bacon**

16 **pork cocktail sausages**

1 **onion**, chopped

1 tablespoon **sunflower oil**

small bunch **sage**, plus extra
to garnish

150 g (5 oz) **fresh
breadcrumbs**

grated rind of 1 **lemon**

1 **egg**, beaten

1.5 kg (3 lb) **whole chicken**

25 g (1 oz) **butter**

salt and **pepper**

For the gravy

2 tablespoons **plain flour**

450 ml (¾ pint) **chicken stock**
(see page 10)

salt and **pepper**

Halve 8 bacon rashers, then wrap a half around each
sausage and set aside.

Fry the onion in the oil for 5 minutes until softened.
Finely chop some of the sage to give about
2 tablespoons. Mix this with the onions, breadcrumbs,
lemon rind, egg and a little seasoning. Shape two-thirds
of the sage stuffing into 8 small balls, then spoon the
remainder into the body cavity of the chicken. Put the
chicken in a roasting tin, cover the breast with the
remaining sage leaves, season and dot with butter,
then arrange the remaining bacon on top.

Cover the chicken loosely with foil, then roast in a
preheated oven, 190°C (375°F), Gas Mark 5, for
1 hour. Remove the foil, baste the chicken and add
the stuffing balls and wrapped sausages to the bottom
of the tin. Roast uncovered for 30–40 minutes until
golden and cooked when tested (see page 11).

Transfer the chicken, stuffing balls and sausages to a
serving plate and keep hot. Pour the fat out of the
roasting tin to leave just the meat juices. Put the pan
on the hob and stir in the flour. Cook for 1 minute, then
gradually mix in the stock, bring to the boil, stirring until
thickened. Season and strain into a jug. Serve with
roast potatoes and vegetables, garnished with sage.

For roast chicken with apricot & walnut stuffing,
omit the sage and lemon rind from the stuffing, adding
the grated rind of ½ orange, 50 g (2 oz) chopped
ready-to-eat dried apricots and 40 g (1½ oz) roughly
chopped walnuts. Tuck 2 bay leaves under the bacon
on the chicken breast in place of the extra sage leaves.

spatchcocked summer poussins

Serves **4**
Preparation time **30 minutes**,
  plus marinating
Cooking time **40 minutes**

grated rind and juice of
  2 **lemons**
7 tablespoons **olive oil**
4 **garlic cloves**, finely
  chopped
4 **poussins**, spatchcocked
  (see page 15)
small bunch **thyme**
4 **courgettes**, thickly sliced
2 **red onions**, cut into wedges
1 **red pepper**, cored,
  deseeded, cut into chunks
1 **yellow pepper**, cored,
  deseeded, cut into chunks
salt and **pepper**

Mix the lemon rind and juice with 4 tablespoons of the oil, the garlic and seasoning. Put the poussins into a large shallow china dish, sprinkle with half the thyme stems, then spoon the lemon mixture over the top. Cover with clingfilm and marinate in the refrigerator for 2 hours (or overnight if possible), turning once.

When ready to cook, thread 2 skewers crossways through each poussin, from the thigh to the wing. Transfer to a large roasting tin and spoon over any marinade. Put all the vegetables into a separate roasting tin with the remaining oil and thyme stems and roast in a preheated oven, 190°C (375°F), Gas Mark 5, for 40 minutes. Turn the vegetables, baste the chicken, and swop oven positions halfway through cooking until the chicken is browned and cooked when tested (see page 11). Transfer to serving plates and serve with warm ciabatta bread.

For soy spatchcocked poussins, mix the grated rind and juice of 1 lemon with the grated rind and juice of 1 lime, 2 tablespoons runny honey, 2 tablespoons dark soy sauce and a 4 cm (1½ inch) piece of grated root ginger. Marinate and cook the poussin as above but without the vegetables, serving instead with salad and new potatoes.

chicken dinner for two

Serves **2**

Preparation time **20 minutes**

Cooking time **47 minutes**

400 g (13 oz) **baking potatoes**, peeled, cut into chunks

1 tablespoon **olive oil**

400 g (13 oz) **butternut squash**, peeled, deseeded, cut into chunks

1 **parsnip**, peeled, cut into quarters

2 boneless, skinless **chicken breasts**, each about 150 g (5 oz)

4 rashers **streaky bacon**

2 **bay leaves**

2 **garlic cloves**, halved

200 ml (7 fl oz) **chicken stock** (see page 10)

salt and **pepper**

Add the potatoes to a saucepan of boiling water and cook for 5 minutes until just tender. Meanwhile, pour the oil into a roasting tin and place in a preheated oven, 200°C (400°F), Gas Mark 6, for 5 minutes.

Drain the potatoes and shake in the colander to rough up their surfaces, then add to the hot oil with the squash and parsnip. Roast for 15 minutes.

Season the chicken breasts and wrap each with 2 rashers of streaky bacon. Turn the vegetables, then add the chicken, bay leaves and garlic to the tin. Roast for 25 minutes until the vegetables are golden and the chicken cooked when tested (see page 11).

Transfer the chicken and vegetables to serving plates. Add the stock to the tin and bring to the boil, scraping up the pan juices. Season and boil for 2 minutes. Pour into a jug and serve with the chicken and vegetables.

For roast chicken with dauphinoise potatoes,

prepare the chicken as above. Blanch 375 g (12 oz) sliced potatoes in boiling water for 4 minutes. Drain and layer in a shallow ovenproof dish with ½ thinly sliced onion, 2 finely chopped garlic cloves and seasoning. Pour over 150 ml (¼ pint) double cream and dot with 15 g (½ oz) butter. Cook on the shelf above the chicken for 30 minutes until golden brown.

roast poussins with orange

Serves **4**
Preparation time **15 minutes**
Cooking time **50 minutes**

4 **poussins**
4 tablespoons **olive oil**
4 stems **rosemary**
1 large **orange**, cut into 8
    wedges
2 **red onions**, cut into wedges
100 g (3½ oz) **marinated
    green and black olives**
2 small **fennel bulbs**, thickly
    sliced
4 rashers **smoked back bacon**
300 ml (½ pint) **chicken stock**
    (see page 10)
salt and **pepper**

Put the poussins into a large roasting tin, drizzle each with ½ tablespoon of oil, then sprinkle with seasoning and the leaves torn from the rosemary stems.

Squeeze the juice from the orange wedges over the top, then put a wedge inside each poussin, adding the rest to the roasting tin with the onion wedges, olives and fennel.

Drape the bacon over the poussin breasts, pour the stock into the base of the roasting tin and drizzle the remaining oil over the vegetables.

Roast in a preheated oven, 190°C (375°F), Gas Mark 5, for 50 minutes, basting and turning the vegetables once during cooking until golden brown and the chicken cooked when tested (see page 11). Transfer to serving plates and serve with warm bread to mop up the pan juices.

For roast poussin with pimenton tomatoes, put the poussins into a roasting tin as above with the oil, seasoning and rosemary. Add 2 red onions, cut into wedges, then 300 g (10 oz) halved cherry tomatoes, 2 chopped garlic cloves and ¼ teaspoon smoked paprika (pimenton) in place of the orange, olives and fennel. Pour over 6 tablespoons red wine, 2 tablespoons balsamic vinegar and some seasoning instead of the stock, and roast as above.

spatchcocked herb poussins

Serves **2**
Preparation time **10 minutes**
Cooking time **25–30 minutes**

2 **poussins**, spatchcocked
  (see page 15)
1 tablespoon **olive oil**
chive flowers, to garnish
  (optional)
salt and **pepper**

For the herb butter
50 g (2 oz) **butter**, softened
1 tablespoon chopped **chives**
1 tablespoon chopped **chervil**
  or **parsley**
1 tablespoon chopped **fennel**
finely grated rind of ½ **lemon**
1 teaspoon **lemon juice**
salt and **pepper**

To make the herb butter, beat together the butter, chives, chervil or parsley, fennel, lemon rind and juice, salt and plenty of pepper.

Season the poussins on both sides and brush them with the oil. Cook by grilling, chargrilling or over the barbecue, turning them several times, until they are cooked through when tested (see page 11), which will take 25–30 minutes.

Transfer to serving plates, top with plenty of herb butter and scatter with chive flowers, if available.

For spatchcocked poussins with blue cheese & chilli butter, mix 50 g (2 oz) butter with 50 g (2 oz) crumbled blue cheese and ¼–½ mild red chilli, deseeded and finely chopped to taste. Prepare the poussins and continue as above.

two meals
from one

chicken & spinach chowder

Serves **6**
Preparation time **15 minutes**
Cooking time **35 minutes**

1 tablespoon **sunflower oil**
25 g (1 oz) **butter**
4 rashers **smoked back bacon**, chopped
2 small **leeks**, thinly sliced, green and white slices separated
750 g (1½ lb) **potatoes**, diced
900 ml (1½ pint) **chicken stock** (see page 10)
150–200 g (5–7 oz) **cooked chicken**, diced
600 ml (1 pint) **semi-skimmed milk**
150 ml (¼ pint) **double cream**
100 g (3½ oz) **spinach**, rinsed, roughly chopped
nutmeg, grated
salt and **pepper**

Heat the oil and butter in a large saucepan, add the bacon, white leeks and diced potatoes and cook over a low heat for 5 minutes, stirring until lightly golden.

Mix in the stock, then bring to the boil, cover and simmer for 20 minutes until the potatoes are just tender. Add the chicken and boil rapidly for 3 minutes.

Stir in the green leeks, milk, cream and a little salt and pepper. Simmer gently for 5 minutes, then stir in the spinach and a little nutmeg. Cook for 2 minutes until the spinach is just cooked.

Ladle into bowls, sprinkle with a little extra nutmeg and serve with crusty bread.

For creamy chicken, bacon & celeriac soup, use 1 chopped onion in place of the leeks and replace the potatoes with celeriac. Fry with the bacon as above. Roughly mash or purée the soup, then add the chicken and cook as above. Mix with cream and nutmeg but omit the spinach, adding 2 tablespoons chopped chives instead.

coconut chicken with noodles

Serves **4**
Preparation time **15 minutes**
Cooking time **20 minutes**

1 tablespoon **sunflower oil**
1 **onion**, finely chopped
2.5 cm (1 inch) piece **root ginger**, grated
2 **garlic cloves**, finely chopped
1 tablespoon **Thai red curry paste**
400 ml (14 fl oz) can **light coconut milk**
150 ml (¼ pint) **chicken stock** (see page 10)
3 teaspoons **fish sauce**
150–200 g (5–7 oz) **cooked chicken**, torn into strips
300 g (10 oz) pack fresh **stir-fry vegetables**
400 g (13 oz) bag fresh **egg noodles**
small bunch **fresh coriander**

Heat the oil in a saucepan. Add the onion, ginger and garlic and fry until pale golden. Stir in the curry paste, then mix in the coconut milk, chicken stock and fish sauce.

Bring to the boil, stir in the chicken, cover and simmer for 15 minutes. Stir in the vegetables and cook for 2 minutes, then add the noodles and the coriander, torn into pieces, and heat until the noodles are piping hot.

Spoon into bowls and serve with chopsticks or a spoon and fork.

For coconut chicken with mixed greens, omit the noodles and ready-prepared stir-fry vegetables and use 300 g (10 oz) mixed sliced pak choi, green beans and broccoli instead. Cook for 4–5 minutes until just tender, then spoon into bowls and serve with rice.

chicken hotchpot

Serves **4**
Preparation time **15 minutes**
Cooking time **45 minutes**

1 tablespoon **sunflower oil**
1 **onion**, roughly chopped
2 small **potatoes**, diced
2 **carrots**, diced
2 small **parsnips**, diced
1 teaspoon **turmeric**
1 tablespoon **mild curry paste**
100 g (3½ oz) **red lentils**
1.2 litres (2 pints) **chicken stock** (see page 10)
100–150 g (3½–5 oz) **cooked chicken**, diced
salt and **pepper**
small bunch **fresh coriander**, to garnish

Heat the oil in a saucepan, add the onion and fry, stirring, until pale golden. Mix in the remaining vegetables and fry for 2–3 minutes. Stir in the turmeric and curry paste, then add the lentils and stock.

Add the chicken and seasoning, then bring to the boil. Cover and simmer for 40 minutes, stirring occasionally, until the vegetables and lentils are softened.

Ladle into bowls and sprinkle with torn coriander leaves. Serve with warm naan breads.

For chicken & barley broth, fry the onion as above, then add the potatoes, carrots and just 1 parsnip, adding 125 g (4 oz) diced swede as well. Omit the turmeric, curry paste and red lentils and add 100 g (3½ oz) pearl barley. Add the stock and chicken as above, then season well, cover and simmer for 1 hour until the barley is tender. Garnish with chopped parsley.

cheat's chicken & chorizo paella

Serves **4**
Preparation time **20 minutes**
Cooking time **25 minutes**

2 tablespoons **olive oil**
1 large **onion**, roughly chopped
150 g (5 oz) **chorizo**, in one
   piece or sliced, peeled, diced
2 **garlic cloves**, finely chopped
1 **red pepper**, cored,
   deseeded, diced
1 **orange pepper**, cored,
   deseeded, diced
4 **tomatoes**, diced
200 g (7 oz) **long-grain**
   white rice
large pinch **smoked paprika**
large pinch **saffron threads**
125–200 g (4–7 oz) **cooked**
   chicken, diced
600–750 ml (1–1¼ pints)
   chicken stock (see page 10)
100 g (3½ oz) **frozen peas**
75 g (3 oz) **marinated mixed**
   olives
3 tablespoons chopped
   parsley (optional)

Heat the oil in a large frying pan, add the onion and chorizo and fry, stirring, until the onion is pale golden. Stir in the garlic, peppers and tomatoes and cook for 2–3 minutes until just softened.

Toss the rice in with the vegetables, then mix in the paprika, saffron, chicken and about half the stock. Bring to the boil, stirring, then cover and simmer for about 20 minutes, topping up with remaining stock as needed.

Stir in the peas and olives and cook until the peas are cooked. Sprinkle with parsley, if liked, and spoon into bowls.

For chicken jambalaya, fry the onion in the oil with 150 g (5 oz) chopped smoked back bacon. Add the garlic, peppers and tomatoes, then mix in the rice. Flavour with 1 teaspoon Cajun spice instead of the paprika and saffron. Add the chicken and stock and simmer until tender. Omit the olives and add 100 g (3½ oz) sliced okra along with the peas at the end.

chicken & lentil pilaff

Serves **4**
Preparation time **15 minutes**
Cooking time **30–35 minutes**

1 tablespoons **olive oil**
1 **onion**, roughly chopped
2–3 **garlic cloves**, finely
  chopped
1 teaspoon **cumin seeds**,
  roughly crushed
2 teaspoons **coriander seeds**,
  roughly crushed
½ teaspoon **ground cinnamon**
400 g (13 oz) can **chopped
  tomatoes**
600–750 ml (1–1¼ pints)
  chicken stock (see
  page 10)
2 teaspoons **dark brown sugar**
100 g (3½ oz) **green lentils**
100 g (3½ oz) easy-cook
  brown rice
100–150 g (3½–5 oz) **cooked
  chicken**, diced
small bunch **mint or fresh
  coriander**, torn, to garnish
50 g (2 oz) **pistachio nuts**,
  halved, to garnish
salt and **pepper**

Heat the oil in the base of a saucepan, add the onion and fry until pale golden. Stir in the garlic and spices and cook for 1 minute, then mix in the tomatoes, 600 ml (1 pint) of the stock and sugar. Stir in the lentils, rice, chicken and seasoning, and bring to the boil. Cover and simmer gently for 30–35 minutes until the rice and lentils are tender, topping up with the remaining stock as needed.

Spoon the pilaff into bowls, top with torn herbs, then sprinkle with the pistachios.

For chicken & bulgar pilaff, fry the onion and garlic in oil as above. Omit the cumin and coriander seeds, using ¼ teaspoon ground allspice instead with the cinnamon. Stir in the tomatoes, stock, sugar and seasoning as above, then mix in 200 g (7 oz) bulgar wheat, a 410 g (13½ oz) can drained borlotti beans and 100–150 g (3½–5 oz) diced cooked chicken. Cover and simmer for 20 minutes. Garnish with lots of chopped parsley.

chicken & avocado salad

Serves **4**
Preparation time **15 minutes**

125 g (4 oz) **light mayonnaise**
2 tablespoons **mango chutney**
grated rind and juice of **1 lime**
2 **avocados**, halved, stoned,
  peeled, diced
4 **spring onions**, thinly sliced
¼ **cucumber**, diced
125–150 g (4–5 oz) **cooked
  chicken**, diced
2 **Little Gem lettuces**
40 g (1½ oz) **mixed salad
  leaves**
small bunch **fresh coriander**,
  optional

Mix the mayonnaise, mango chutney and lime rind together in a large bowl. Toss the lime juice with the avocados, then add to the dressing. Add the spring onions, cucumber and chicken and fold the mixture together lightly so that it is semi-mixed.

Divide the lettuce leaves between 4 serving plates and top with the other salad leaves. Spoon over the chicken salad and garnish with torn coriander leaves, if liked. Serve immediately.

For chicken Waldorf salad, mix the same quantity of mayonnaise with the grated rind of ½ lemon, tossing the juice with 2 cored and diced dessert apples. Add the apples to the dressing along with 40 g (1½ oz) sultanas, 4 stems celery, thickly sliced, and 125–150 g (4–5 oz) diced cooked chicken. Serve on salad leaves as above, omitting the coriander.

cheesy chicken & chutney puffs

Makes **9**
Preparation time **30 minutes**
Cooking time **20 minutes**

100 g (3½ oz) **cooked
  chicken**, diced
75 g (3 oz) **tomatoes**, diced
50 g (2 oz) **frozen sweetcorn**,
  defrosted
3 tablespoons **tomato
  chutney**
50 g (2 oz) **mature Cheddar
  cheese**, grated
500 g (1 lb) chilled **puff pastry**
flour, for rolling
1 **egg**, beaten

Mix the chicken, tomatoes, sweetcorn and chutney together, then stir in two-thirds of the cheese.

Roll out half the pastry on a lightly floured surface and trim to a 30 cm (12 inch) square. Brush with the egg, then spoon the filling over the pastry in 9 evenly spaced mounds.

Roll out the remaining pastry until a little larger than the first layer, then place it over the other pastry square. Gently press down around the filling, then cut into 9 squares with a knife or pastry wheel. Transfer to an oiled baking sheet.

Brush the tops with a little more beaten egg, sprinkle with the remaining cheese and bake in a preheated oven, 200°C (400°F), Gas Mark 6, for 20 minutes until well risen and golden. Serve warm or cold with salad.

For cheesy chicken & spinach puffs, mix the cooked chicken with 100 g (3½ oz) low-fat cream cheese with garlic and herbs and 150 g (5 oz) frozen leaf spinach, defrosted and well drained. Season well with salt, pepper and a little grated nutmeg. Dot the filling over the rolled-out pastry and continue as above.

curried chicken & couscous salad

Serves **4**
Preparation time **15 minutes**

200 g (7 oz) **couscous**
50 g (2 oz) **sultanas**
2 teaspoons **mild curry paste**
450 ml (¾ pint) **boiling water**
2 **tomatoes**, diced
½ **green, red** or **yellow pepper**,
  cored, deseeded, diced
½ **red onion**, finely chopped
small bunch **fresh coriander**,
  finely chopped
40 g (1½ oz) lightly toasted
  desiccated coconut
125–175 g (4–6 oz) **cooked
  chicken**, diced
grated rind and juice of **1 lime**
3 tablespoons **sunflower oil**
salt and **pepper**

Put the couscous, sultanas and curry paste into a large
bowl, add the boiling water and mix together. Leave to
stand for 5 minutes.

Fluff up the couscous with a fork, then mix in the
tomatoes, pepper, onion, coriander, coconut and chicken.

Mix the lime rind and juice with the oil and a little
seasoning. Add to the couscous and toss together.
Spoon into bowls and serve.

For minted lemon couscous, omit the curry paste
and add 2 teaspoons harissa paste when soaking the
couscous and sultanas in boiling water. Stir in ½ green
pepper, cored, deseeded and diced, 4 chopped
spring onions, 50 g (2 oz) sliced pistachio nuts and
3 tablespoons each chopped mint and parsley, plus
the chicken as above. Make up a dressing with the
grated rind and juice of ½ lemon, 3 tablespoons olive
oil and seasoning.

mini chicken & broccoli frittatas

Makes **12**
Preparation time **15 minutes**
Cooking time **15 minutes**

250 g (8 oz) **broccoli**, cut into
small florets
oil, for greasing
125–150 g (4–5 oz) **cooked
chicken**, diced
6 **eggs**
125 ml (4 fl oz) **milk**
40 g (1½ oz) **Parmesan
cheese**, freshly grated
salt and **pepper**

Add the broccoli to a saucepan of boiling water and
cook for 3 minutes, then drain into a colander. Brush
the insides of a 12-section nonstick muffin tin with a
little oil, then divide both the broccoli and the chicken
between the sections.

Beat the eggs, milk and Parmesan together in a jug,
season generously, then pour the mixture over the
broccoli and chicken.

Bake in a preheated oven, 190°C (375°F), Gas Mark
5, for 15 minutes until well risen and golden. Loosen
the edges of the frittatas, then turn out and serve with
a tomato salad or baked beans.

For chicken, bacon & red onion frittata, heat
1 tablespoon olive oil in a medium frying pan, add
125 g (4 oz) diced streaky bacon and 1 sliced red
onion and fry for 5 minutes until golden. Add
125–150 g (4–5 oz) diced cooked chicken and fry
until piping hot. Beat the eggs and milk together,
then season. Add an extra 1 tablespoon oil to the
pan, then pour in the egg mixture. Fry until the
underside is golden, then finish off under a hot grill
until set and golden. Cut into wedges to serve.

index

acknowledgements

Executive editor: Nicola Hill
Editor: Ruth Wiseall
Executive art editor: Sally Bond
Designer: Claire Dale for Cobalt Id
Photographer: David Munns
Home economist: Sara Lewis
Prop stylist: Liz Hippisley
Senior production controller: Amanda Mackie

Special photography: © Octopus Publishing Group Limited/David Munns. **Other photography**: © Octopus Publishing Group Limited/67, 69; /Bill Reavell 95; /David Loftus 87; /Ian Wallace 75, 91; /Lis Parsons 37, 65; /Sean Myers 41, 45, 51, 55, 63, 99, 103, 107, 157, 163, 167, 175; /Stephen Conroy 113, 215; /William Lingwood 33, 83, 205.

The publisher would like to thank David Mellor (4 Sloane Square, London SW1W 8EE, 0207 730 7240, www.davidmellordesign.co.uk) for the loan of kitchen equipment, plates and cutlery.